To. Shura

From. Peter duin-Brown

19/11/09

House of Lachasse

The Story of a Very English Gentleman

HOUSE OF LACHASSE

The Story of a Very English Gentleman

Peter Lewis-Crown OBE

DELANCEY PRESS
LONDON 2009

Published by Delancey Press Ltd.
23 Berkeley Square
London W1J 6HE

www.delanceypress.com

A CIP catalogue record for this title is available from the British Library.

First published 2009

Edited by Amy Spencer
Jacket by e-Digital Design
Typeset by BookType
Printed and bound by TJ International Ltd.

ISBN 978 1 907205 13 2

House of Lachasse documents the past seventy years of British fashion through the life of one designer. It tells the story of Peter Lewis-Crown as his life becomes entwined with the history of one of London's leading couture houses. It is a celebration of beautiful clothes, the talented people who design them and the lucky people who wear them.

Peter Lewis-Crown's association with Lachasse is an object lesson in the rewards of dedication and hard work. As a boy he showed artistic talent and entrepreneurial flair. He developed into a man with a passionate determination to succeed in the fiercely competitive world of haute couture, and success came as he rose to head up one of London's premier fashion houses.

In the early days the house style of Lachasse was hugely influenced by the iconic figures of Digby Morton, Hardy Amies and Michael Donellan. Later Lachasse developed their own style and dressed many of the country's most elegant women for the most glamorous events in the social calendar. Peter Lewis-Crown's story is engagingly embroidered with anecdote, and flavoured with an insider's view of the colourful personalities that populate the world of fashion. He takes us behind the scenes at high society fashion shows, tells us what it is like to dress royalty and shares with us the mysteries of design from cutting-room to catwalk. His passion illuminates the narrative and we are never left in doubt about the hard work and commitment involved.

Beyond the fashion scene Peter Lewis-Crown has lived a full and satisfying life. He has used his talents and inspiration generously in support of many worthy causes and has earned the affection and respect in which he is justly held.

His story comes full circle with the closing of Lachasse, one of the longest surviving fashion houses, and leaves us with the question 'where does fashion go from here?'

Dame Norma Major DBE
September 2009

The past may be a foreign country where things are done differently, but so is the world of *Haute Couture*, a kingdom of rules and shibboleths and dangers unknown to lesser mortals.

In his delightful memoir, *House of Lachasse*, Peter Lewis Crown undertakes to reveal, and to guide us through, this exotic territory, where the characters of both the flamboyant, designers and the frequently demanding and often impossible clients, are all as colourful as the stuff from which those wonderful clothes were made.

Ultimately, the book provides a kindly view of these shenanigans, the clue being in the sub-title, *The Story of a Very English Gentleman*, and it is sometimes hard to understand how a man with the courteous and gentle instincts of a diffident, manorial lord, can have survived among the savage, flesh-eating beasts of this particular jungle, but it only makes the journey warmer and more satisfying.

Of course, Crown is dealing here with a world which, if not quite lost, has become the demesne of a brasher, newer group, and viewed through the lens of his charming and comfortable prose it is difficult not to feel a twang of nostalgia for those imperious great ladies who made life so hard, yet so rewarding, for this particular gentleman in the London of half a century ago. Even for those who do not lament the changes that have curtailed the pleasures of those "born to rule," this is a memorable account of a way of life, and a way of thinking, that always boasted plenty of real style.

Julian Fellowes
September 2009

Acknowledgements

I would like to express my sincere thanks to all the people in my life who have helped and supported me in achieving my ambitions, to those who have contributed to the book and to its readers. I hope that you will all find my story interesting, informative and, at times, amusing.

Table of Contents

A brief history of Lachasse from its founding in 1928 to the present day: people who worked there. How it developed into an iconic couture house.

Peter Lewis-Crown's early family life in Hunstanton, from idyllic days spent on the beach to the outbreak of World War Two. We are introduced to the fashion of the era as seen through the eyes of a young boy in a small town.

Lewis-Crown starts attending the grammar school and his horizons begin to broaden. He is soon dreaming of London and the fashion world. This chapter focuses on the young Lewis-Crown's burgeoning creativity and ingenuity as he starts to sell his handmade crafts to raise money for charity.

Lewis-Crown realises a boyhood dream and buys a motorbike. He recalls his feelings about the new sense of freedom he experiences and reflects on his life.

In this final chapter, Lewis-Crown discusses the changing world of fashion and makes predictions about what new trends will come next.

Introduction

Although it was never my ambition to have my name in lights or over the door of a business, I was delighted to become part of the history of Lachasse, one of London's best loved couture houses. The satisfaction I have found in my career and the joy of seeing my creations come to life have been remarkable. I have enjoyed my life and found loyal friends across the world who have generously shared their successes and lifestyles with me.

I have written this book for everyone with an interest in fashion and particularly for students hoping to enter the fashion industry. It is important to remember that working in fashion is not always glamorous and exciting. It is hard work and only complete devotion will help you succeed. Once reaching the top of the trade, the work does not stop but there are social rewards and you can earn a living. You can find success, as I did, regardless of your background but you must be prepared to work hard.

I dressed many people through my long career and, whether they were royalty or had saved up for a Lachasse garment, I gave each one a sense of confidence. I believe that if you care about your clothes and appearance then it gives inner confidence to you and joy to other people.

I hope that you will enjoy my book and the ride through my life.

Peter Lewis-Crown
London, 2009

Chapter One

The History of Lachasse

To understand the position that Lachasse held in the couture world and in the hearts of its clients, we must first look back at its beginnings. In 1928, two entrepreneurial women, Mrs Philips and Miss Gray, had an extraordinary idea. They knew that most women were buying their expensive clothes in Paris or at the few established dressmakers and tailors in Mayfair, and wanted to offer them an alternative. They had the idea of opening a different kind of business, selling less expensive clothes and focusing on soft tweed dresses and suits. The clothes were to be well made and original but needed fewer fittings than the haute couture garments being made by the main fashion houses. They wanted to introduce a new look to women in London.

They took their idea to Mr Shingleton, who owned property in Mayfair, to see if he had any premises suitable for their business. He saw the potential in their idea and offered to house them in his property in Bond Street and join them in business. The two women readily agreed to his offer and to the prime location. They moved in, opened their business, which they called Gray, Paulette & Shingleton, and quickly gained the support of their friends and developed a burgeoning clientèle. The business partnership started off successfully and it wasn't too long before Mr Shingleton and Miss Gray were married. The business grew steadily and they moved to larger premises in Berkeley Square, the once town residence of Admiral Congreave.

In 1929, the business took a new turn. A young man named Digby Morton, who had been doing sketches for Gray, Paulette & Shingleton, was given the job of designer. He became well-known for his use of Donegal tweeds for suits, coats and day dresses and began to develop a new aesthetic for the business, one which focused on simple outdoor and sportswear. He experimented with traditional fabrics and colours but created something quite different. His clothes quickly became very fashionable for London ladies as an alternative to what Paris had to offer. With this bold new direction, it was time that Gray, Paulette & Shingleton had a new name. Mr Morton suggested 'Lachasse', meaning 'the hunt' in French. This name captured a sense of fashion for an elegant outdoor life and seemed perfect. He designed a logo for Lachasse and his black and white colour scheme has been used ever since.

There were soon more changes at Lachasse. In the spring of 1929, Mr Todd, who had once been a tailor before training in Paris, joined the company as its tailor and Miss Joyce became the dressmaker. She was small in stature but made up for it in her vitality. As a team, they became the best in the West End. Lachasse was a great success.

Mr Morton stayed with Lachasse until 1934, when he decided to open his own fashion house in Palace Gate under his own name. His contract stipulated that he must not start his business anywhere near Lachasse, so he stayed in Palace Gate for many years until he eventually moved to Bourdon Hill, just off Berkeley Square.

In 1939, disaster hit Lachasse and its premises were shattered by a German bomb. By this time, Lachasse had become so successful that the Directors, who by now included several members of the Shingleton family, realised that they needed to find a larger building and so took a lease from Lord Rosebery on stables on Farm Street. This lease came with two unusual conditions. The first was that virtually no changes could be made to the inside or the outside of the building. The second was that Lachasse has to supply a nearby mews house for Lord Rosebery's chauffeur and car. This condition lasted until 1969 when everyone realised that the mews house and garage had not been used for many years and so were no longer needed.

The board of Lachasse began looking for a new designer and

it was a Mrs Amies who suggested that her son, Hardy Amies, might be interested in a career in the fashion trade. He had been working for Avery, the weighing machine firm, and was looking for a change. Mr Shingleton had read a letter written by Hardy Amies, where he had described a dress worn by Mrs Shingleton at a hunt ball, and was impressed by the way he wrote about fashion. He decided to give the young man a chance and offered him the job of second male designer. Straight away, Mr Amies began to experiment with tailoring. Under the guidance of Mr Todd, Mr Amies created suits and clothes based on geometric lines. He tried a new approach to tailoring. He played with the way material was cut and, instead of creating stripes that ran vertically to the body, his often ran horizontally around it. This took a great deal of work to match all the seams but the result was always creatively stylish and a new look in tailoring was born.

Mr Amies was committed to Lachasse and his new career in fashion but, in 1940, he was called up for war service and became a paratrooper. Whenever he came home on leave, he spent all his time designing collections for the women who had saved their clothing coupons to spend on his original designs. When the War ended, Mr Amies returned to take up his post as designer at Lachasse. However, like all young designers he longed to have his own business and, in late 1945, left to open his own house in Saville Row.

There were to be more changes at Lachasse and, in 1946, a new board was formed, made up of Mr Shingleton, Mr Ernest Shingleton, Mr Todd, Miss Joyce and Miss Greenwood, the head of millinery. Two years later, Mr Shingleton retired and Miss Greenwood took over as Managing Director. In 1949, I joined Lachasse. It was a small step for such a famous and long estab-lished fashion house but a major step in my career path.

There was still no head designer in place and so the new board set to work to find a suitable designer to follow the elegant, popular and talented Mr Amies. It was a struggle to find anyone suitable until a friend of Miss Joyce suggested another unknown young man. This time, it was a medical student who had also served in the Royal Artillery who was looking for a break into the couture end of the fashion trade. His name was Michael Donellan, later to be known as Mr Michael, and he impressed the board so much that they offered him the job as the new designer.

It was the Coronation Year of 1953 when Mr Michael joined Lachasse, when Britain had the time, reason and money to indulge itself after the War and was celebrating the arrival of Queen Elizabeth II. Mr Michael gave people what they wanted. He was an experimental designer with big ideas. He soon made the Lachasse suit internationally famous when he found a design, fabric and colour that could be worn around the clock and at any occasion. Women flocked to Lachasse and the staff grew to 134. Collection showings became like first nights at the theatre and at each one a new look for suits was unveiled.

Mr Michael found much of his inspiration for his designs in his muse – a mannequin named Avril Humphries. She had been working in a store in Bedfordshire when she answered an advertisement for a job as a mannequin and quickly progressed to become Lachasse's head mannequin. With her small bone structure, dark close-cropped hair and pixie smile, Avril became known as 'Miss Perfection' and was the delight of photographers and fashion writers around the globe.

In the post-war years, Lachasse was not the only fashion house in Farm Street. Dale Cavahnaugh had one at No.27a and he was one of the most *avant garde* designers for men, well ahead of his time. In August 1948, he launched his Bold Look as a counter blast to Dior's New Look for women, which had given women a chance to look feminine again after years of wartime austerity. Dale Cavahnaugh certainly left a mark on men's fashion at the time. He, together with Vince, who opened a men's boutique in Carnaby Street in the '50s, was probably one of the greatest influences on the clothes that men are wearing today.

Mr Michael did not stay at Lachasse for long. He soon became restless and wanted to change the name of the business to his own. Mr Singleton refused and so Mr Michael left in a fury to open his own house. He later took over the business of Peter Russell in Carlos Place, where he remained for several years making his world-famous suits, coats and dresses until it closed at the end of June 1971.

At the time of Michael's departure, Miss Greenwood was in America on a business trip so it fell to Miss Joyce and Mr Todd to start looking for a new designer. They suggested to me that I should prepare sketches for the collection, so of course I worked day and night to prepare a full sketch book. The overpowering Miss Greenwood arrived back from her trip, looked at my sketches, and said that, at 22 years old, I was far too young and inexperienced to take on the mantle of designer at Lachasse and so the search went on.

The atmosphere at Lachasse was gloomy and depressing. After the glamour and publicity of the past era, suddenly everything had come to a full stop and Lachasse was struggling to keep up its reputation. Interviews took place but no suitable designer could be found. Then, out of the blue, Marquis Mac-Swinney of Mashanaglass arrived in London with his sketches. He had a wide knowledge of the fashion trade both in Britain and America and his art work was impeccable.

At once, Miss Greenwood proposed that he should be the next designer at Lachasse. He became known as Mr Owen, one of his many first names, and he set at once to create a collection to be praised as highly as those of his distinguished predecessors. He rose to the occasion and, despite the fact that several of the staff had followed Mr Michael when he left, a collection was made and shown.

During his reign as designer at Lachasse, Mr Owen was responsible for several garments that caught the attention of the media. In December 1954, he dyed three seven-guinea Irish linen damask tablecloths a brilliant sapphire blue and made them into a suit. This not only caused a stir in the fashion world but the suit was shown to the Queen Mother and Princess Margaret at a fashion show.

Mr Owen stayed with Lachasse for many years as its last official designer. At the same time, he took on freelance work for international companies, such as Jantzen, the swimwear manufacturers, and wrote a book. The amount of freelance work he took on grew and when I began to design for my own clientèle he was able to travel more. His wife, son and step-daughter lived in Germany and he found himself pulled in several directions at once. Gradually, he came less and less to Lachasse and eventually came simply to work on the collections twice a year.

During Mr Owen's period as designer, a young man educated at Canterbury School came for an interview. Everyone could see his potential and Clive was employed, first of all in the office, then as a general assistant to Mr Owen and later he was allowed to do some of the designing for the collection. He was immensely ambitious and left the house in 1963 to open his own fashion house on George Street. He succeeded for several years, backed by the Dowager Lady Alvingham, before sadly closing when steeply rising costs forced him out of business. In May 1983, he began a completely new venture, opening a wine bar in Covent Garden called Charlie Bubbles.

I had found my true place at Lachasse as a *vendeur*, or salesman, and by the '60s I was creating my own designs for my clients. This was one of the most exciting times for me as I became more and more responsible for Lachasse's future. Over the years, I had been secretly buying shares in Lachasse. Mr Shingleton recognised my talent and wanted to keep me loyal to the business so, in the '60s, he insisted that members of his family sold me their shares and I soon found myself owning one third of the business. When Miss Joyce retired, she left me her third of the business and I became Chairman. I began to feel more secure about my future and gave up all my ideas about leaving and opening my own business. I was completely satisfied at Lachasse.

The Directors thought it best that none of the employees knew that I had shares in the business, especially the four senior women in the showroom. It was a very difficult time for me as I was desperate to speak out but thought that my colleagues would have been jealous. On 1st January1964, I was appointed Director of Lachasse and the fact that I had considerable shares in the company was no longer a secret. The news was announced at a staff party and, to my surprise, everyone generously drank to my health and success. When Mr Todd retired in 1970, after succeeding Miss Greenwood as Chairman, I bought his shares in the business and so I was in the exciting position of being the sole owner of Lachasse. It was the end of an era for the House of Lachasse and I was left in change of operating the business with the secretary and small shareholder Miss Young. I now found myself serving all the clients, designing the clothes, and, with Lily the milliner, making the hats as well.

During this period of great change in Lachasse's history, I was slowly being prepared for new responsibilities and the business was evolving. Many famous names began to join Lachasse and share its premises. The first of these partnerships began in 1962, when Austrian milliner Madame Emmy Gruder, known as Madame Mariva, closed her business in Beauchamp Place and brought her staff and clients to Lachasse. Madame Brill, another Austrian milliner who had left her native country in 1938, also came to Lachasse in 1971. Sadly the two ladies, both with strong artistic temperaments, could not agree and Madame Brill soon left to continue her work elsewhere.

In 1966, Angele Delange, who had made her name designing elegant dresses and wedding gowns at her premises in Bruton Mews, came to Lachasse. The day-to-day running of her own business had proved too much for her artistic temperament and so she brought her staff and clients to us, where there was plenty of space and clients. This arrangement worked well for several years until she was taken ill, went on holiday to Germany and sadly died there. I learned a great deal from Angele, who draped her gowns, tied bows that looked like butterflies and handled soft fabrics with a masterful touch.

When the lease of her own premises ended in 1975, yet another new name joined us – Madam Adele. Renowned since the '40s for hats and dresses, she was reluctant to retire and so she came to Lachasse. We made a separate department for her, where her clients could buy her ready-to-wear clothes and hats and, if they wished, ensembles from Lachasse at the same time.

When Madame Adele eventually decided to retire to Brighton, I took over buying the ready-to-wear collection. This was not only a new responsibility but also an exciting challenge. I had only ever experienced the couture world until then and began to see what women wanted as we moved into the 1980s, with its rapidly changing pattern of life. By then, many women didn't have the time, need or finance for increasingly expensive couture clothes and instead chose to dress in a practical but elegant way. I found myself working on the two main collections each year as well as buying for the ready-to-wear department, which reflected the same colours and lines of the more expensive clothes but without the superior quality and detail. Clients began to choose several couture garments each season and then complete their wardrobes with ready-to-wear pieces, on which we provided any alterations free of charge.

This new direction in the history of Lachasse led to some exciting partnerships with leading fashion labels of the day. In the 1960s, we were asked by Pringles of Scotland to design a new style of cardigan. It was a huge success and, as soon as it was launched, the orders started to pour in. Clients ordered the cardigans through the post, giving them a choice of colour and style. When they were ready, they were posted to Lachasse and then on to the client. The partnership was extremely successful and helped to advertise our services to a huge number of potential clients.

A younger set of clients began to turn to Lachasse. At first, they came looking for Ascot and wedding hats and then gradually came to us for their clothing as well. When they became brides, they had their dresses made in the couture part of the business and often bought their trousseaux from the ready-to-wear section. With our new surge in popularity, turnover leapt and our client list grew to 7,000 and when faced with a massive rent increase in 1983 we were able somehow to meet it.

With all my new responsibilities came new challenges. In 1985, Lachasse's landlord decided not to renew the lease on Farm Street so I had the difficult task of looking for new premises. For weeks, Miss Young and I walked the streets of Mayfair looking for a suitable property. Each weekend, I trudged through the area on what became a desperate hunt. The new premises had to be unique and elegant for our clients and suitable for our team of workers, who, like the clients, had all pledged to follow us. As the months went by, we realised that this wasn't going to be an easy task.

At the time, we had a loyal client who lived in St Mary Abbots Court in Kensington. She was becoming less mobile and so I and the fitters often went to her flat before Lachasse opened for the day to do her fittings. On one such morning, road works had caused heavy traffic jams and we were stuck. As we slowly passed Thurloe Place, I noticed a large To Let sign hanging in the window of a shop that had once been the Romanian Tourist Office. It was an attractive, well positioned building and so I took a note of the details.

As soon as I returned to Lachasse later than morning, I made arrangements to view the premises. When we reached it, keys in hand, we realised that it didn't look so good up close. To describe the building as a mess would be putting it mildly. The shop front had a cracked pane of glass with an unmistakable bullet hole in the centre. The white marble front steps had been used by the homeless as a make-shift bed.

But, the moment we opened the door, Miss Young looked at me and said, 'This is what we have been looking for.'

The mezzanine floor had a picture frame entrance and led to a studio room at the rear. There were steps down to the basement, where we found a dump of unimaginable rubbish and four well-lit large rooms, one leading out to a small courtyard. It was perfect. I could almost imagine it full of the bustling activity of Lachasse, with the happy chatter of clients and *vendeurs* during fittings and the workers in the busy workrooms.

We agreed to take the lease. Now the real work began and time was fast running out. Lawyers were instructed to arrange the details and builders were hired and given precise instructions about what to do. Negotiations with the landlord took a long time and we were given the keys only four weeks before we had to move from Farm Street. Most of the details were left to the capable Miss Young as I had to finish the orders and clear out our junk-filled cupboards, while maintaining a sense of calm elegance for our clients.

Somehow, everything was finished and on a Saturday morning in January 1986 large removal vans arrived at Farm Street. Soon, we were speeding our way around Hyde Park Corner with 4 Farm Street behind us and 29 Thurloe Place ahead. By noon, the vans were unpacked and we were nearly ready to open. We just had to put up the black Lachasse sign above the shop front, which we had painted pristine white. On Monday morning, all the workers arrived to find their work and all the necessary tools in place on their work tables. By 10am, our first client arrived with a basket of food and wine and good luck omens such as salt, coins and bread to insure that we would be blessed.

Lachasse prospered in Thurloe Place, the client list grew and other fashion businesses followed our success and moved nearby. As the years past, many of the main Lachasse staff began to reach retirement age and a few sadly died. There were countless people desperate to work at Lachasse but I began to feel that I was too old to start training new people. The rent on our premises increased and it became clear that it was an end of an era for Lachasse and for the wider couture world. The world was rapidly changing and there seemed to be less need for elegant clothing in the lives of most people. It was with great sadness that I decided to close Lachasse at the end of October 2007. It was a very difficult decision. Lachasse was not just a business with a rich history and a place in the heart of the London couture world, it was also my life.

Chapter Two

Boyhood

Life for me began on April 18th 1930 at midday. It was Good Friday and I was born in Hunstanton, a small seaside town in Norfolk. While the rest of the country experienced great social change, Hunstanton was a quiet haven. It was the perfect place for childhood adventures. My mother worked for a department store in Hunstanton and later for a large store in Norwich as a fashion buyer for the gown department, and my father was a barber. I already had a five year old brother called Richard and my sister, Patricia, arrived exactly thirteen months later. Patricia and I were close from the start. I protected her when she got into trouble and she joined me in all my adventures. We were inseparable.

Before we started at the local school, we were allowed to roam the beach that lay about a hundred yards from our own garden over a railway bridge. There wasn't an inch of it that we didn't know, from the wavy shoreline to the rolling sand dunes. We spent most days dancing on the seaweed-covered rocks, vaulting with poles from rock to rock and gathering winkles and crabs. Our brother made us kites from coloured cellophane and we flew them on the salty breezes. On hot summer days, we rushed our chores and ran to watch the Punch and Judy show held at mid-day on the beach. We sat on the promenade with our feet dangling over the edge and watched Mr Punch and his wife Judy fight the crocodile, aided by the policeman. Once a year, the Daily Mail newspaper held a sand castle building competition and Patricia and I wandered the beach gathering the finest seaweed, shells, pebbles and rocks for our sand castle designs. The beach was one of the first places where I began to experiment with my creativity.

When we were not roaming the beach we were playing on our grandfather's dairy farm with our many cousins. The land is now a housing estate but, during the long summers of my childhood, it was a wonderful spot for playing cowboys and Indians and cops and robbers. Dressing up was an essential part of my childhood. I loved costumes and clothes and was always pretending to be different characters. One of my earliest hobbies was to play dressing up with my friends, who regularly came to play in our garden. My mother let us use her old clothes and handmade fancy dress outfits and from these we created any costume imaginable. She also gave us a wind up gramophone and we played her records over and over in the open air. We were forbidden from leaving the garden unaccompanied but we always found a way to sneak out of the gate for a parade around the nearby streets. If Mother caught us, as she often did, Patricia and I would be scolded and our friends sent home.

In the early '30s, life was idyllic. Our small seaside town had a great sense of community and the whole town joined together for social occasions and celebrations. Patricia and I always entered the annual fancy dress parades and often won. My mother bought fancy dress pattern books and then, after a great deal of thought and long consultations with my father, fittings began. There was an air of secrecy surrounding our costumes because Mother never told us in advance what they were going to be. While my parents worked late into the night on our costumes, we children tried to imagine what they were creating. My mother had such a wonderful imagination and often cleverly designed the outfits to represent current events and popular advertisements of the day. From sackcloth dyed black with large white spots and twine, I became the horse from an advert for Cough Zubes. From white card and blackout curtains, my mother and her friends became the symbol of Three Nuns Tobacco.

I began to notice clothes at a young age. The colours and cuts fascinated me. Even in my small town, I managed to find plenty to interest me. As a choirboy, I watched the congregation every

14

Sunday to glimpse the latest colours and clothes. After church, the walk home along the promenade was a fashion parade. Everyone, from farm workers to businessmen, dressed up on a Sunday. At that time, Hunstanton was one of the most elegant seaside resorts in the country. People rented local houses for the summer and brought their staff with them. Out of season, it wasn't unusual to see Queen Mary shopping at Marshalls in the High Street or walking with members of the royal family along the promenade. I was always desperate to see what colours and designs they were wearing.

One Sunday, I spotted a very elegant woman walking along dressed in a white and red dress with a red newspaper print over it. It was very *avant guarde* for the '30s and I was thrilled and rushed home to describe the outfit to my mother, who was as excited as I was about new fashions. She was from an elegant family and I can still clearly see Grandma elegantly dressed with long frocks, high frilled collars and her hair pulled high on her head. One Aunt was noted for her stylish large brimmed hats. They were so large that she was often forced to turn sideways when entering a house. My taste and awareness for colour and style was awakened in my childhood. I took inspiration from all around me and soon began to experiment with creating my own fashion designs, often recreating the clothes I saw for Patricia's dolls.

The Second World War changed Hunstanton and family life. There were blackouts and rationing and troops soon began to outnumber the local people. Our beautiful beach was out of bounds with mines and barbed wire everywhere. Hunstanton, a coastal town with a constant threat of invasion, was a garrison town during the War and movement in and out of the area was restricted. Home life soon became very unsettled. My father was called up at the beginning of the War and my brother Richard left home to work in Surrey, at Vickers aircraft works. My mother, sister and I were left at home. Just before my father left, he sat me on the kitchen table and told me I was now to be the man of the house. I had new responsibilities forced upon me and I was still only nine years old.

We had to close down my father's hairdressing business while he was away. My mother was very resourceful and, to support the family, she opened a general store just down the road from our house and served teas and cakes to troops stationed in the town. She even worked out how to replicate a famous brand of hair cream and sold it by the bottle. My sister and I helped by forming a little production line and filling the bottles and glued on the labels.

It always amazed me how people followed fashion during wartime. Life was difficult but they still wanted to look their best. They copied fashions, exchanged clothes and made do with what they had available. Both men and women imitated the set look of the day as seen in the top fashion houses, newspapers and magazines. Each season, there was a new hairstyle and shoes. Many women surrendered their clothing coupons to the main fashion houses to be kept until they had saved enough for a particular garment. When the wedge-heeled shoe came into fashion, people saved their coupons for a pair just so they could be seen wearing the latest look. Hats were not rationed so, when all else failed, women turned to the milliner for inspiration. Knitting your own garments was also popular, as wool was not rationed. Everyone was always knitting a jumper or a cardigan from the latest patterns and knitting garments for the Forces. Knitted berets with pom-poms and matching scarves and gloves were a popular way to use up left over yarn. Every scrap of available fabric was used to make clothes. Old curtains were transformed into dresses, morning suits were re-cut into town suits and underwear was made from old parachute silks.

When I started at the local school, my artistic talent was noticed by my teachers and my formal art training began. The headmaster's wife picked out three pupils who she believed showed outstanding promise and gave them private drawing lessons out of school hours. I was one of these lucky ones. She encouraged us to enter the competitions run by the National Savings campaigns, as well as local competitions held in aid of the war effort. Although my artistic skills were still limited, there was plenty to nourish my developing imagination. I started to notice art and architecture all around me and went to exhibitions held in the local shops and in Norwich and King's Lynn, a nearby market town. It was on these outings to King's Lynn that I first saw the King Edward VII Grammar School, a large red brick building with vast playing fields. From the moment I set eyes on it, I knew I wanted to be one of its smartly dressed pupils; but first it meant passing the Scholarship examination.

When I was nine, my father came home on leave and I noticed that he and my mother seemed to be secretly discussing something. I often saw them talking but they fell silent when I approached. After my father had gone back, my mother made several journeys into King's Lynn and raced to collect the post whenever the postman called. At first, I assumed that she was waiting for a letter from my father but it seemed that she was looking for something else. One evening, she sat me down and asked if I had really set my mind on going to the grammar school. My answer left her in no doubt as to my determination. She told me that the next day I was to go shopping in King's Lynn with her and Patricia. When we got there, I was taken instead to King Edward VII School and, after being introduced to the headmaster, I was shown into a hall where about thirty other nine-year old boys sat in nervous anticipation. We were led to a small building, seated at separate desks and given papers. As I turned mine over, I realised that it was the entrance exam and I was hit with a wave of excitement and terror. This was what I had dreamed of for so long, for years in fact. Now, I understood that my parents were prepared to make sacrifices in order to pay for me to go to the school – as long as I could pass the exam.

I took the exam and felt like a champion. It must have been my lucky day, for a few weeks later my mother told me with pride that I had passed, along with several of my friends, and that I would be starting at my new school in the autumn term. Although clothes were strictly rationed during the War, my mother somehow managed to get enough coupons together for my new school uniform. I felt very proud as I tried on the grey trousers, red blazer and black lace-up shoes and the dark charcoal two-piece suit for special occasions. I was ready and now had only to wait until September to begin my new adventures.

Chapter Three

School Days

In September 1944, I started my new life at the Grammar School. I had to catch a bus early every morning, alongside business people travelling to work, to make the sixteen mile journey to King's Lynn. Although it was the responsibility of the senior boys and prefects to keep us in order, they stayed out of the way on the top deck. I suspect they were often having a forbidden cigarette, while we *enfants terribles* terrorised the lower deck. At the least sign of noise, they descended upon us to sort out any problems. Our punishment was usually 100 lines, which had to be done overnight and handed in the following morning.

At school, my work at first left much to be desired. Sport did not appeal to me and I was not sorry when a doctor said that I could not play football or cricket in case I fell and injured my already weak back. I was, however, allowed to swim and this proved to be the only sport at which I did well and I won many certificates. In place of the field sports, I worked in the school garden as part of the wartime Grow More Food campaign. Our neat little vegetable patch stretched alongside the railway line. As the trains steamed past, we put down our tools and waved to the friendly passengers. The food we grew kept the school canteen supplied with vegetables. It was ironic considering how much I hated the unpalatable school food.

In class, I muddled along. While I excelled at art under the guidance of the art mistress Evelyn Sheldon, my maths let me down so it was suggested that I should have some private lessons. I made the best of this by striking a bargain. I would agree to extra maths lessons if I could also have private art lessons. I loved these art lessons and the chance to experiment with colour and form and put up with the maths as a necessary evil. Guided and encouraged by my tutor, I began to take art more seriously. My school results improved gradually but art remained my real passion. I entered every art competition I could find and often won. I was not so successful at maths. Eventually the mathematics master told me, during one of my private lessons, that he doubted that I would ever grasp the principles of his subject and suggested I give it up completely. My mother refused to allow me to stop and so the master and I reached a compromise. I continued to go to his house for maths lessons but, instead of learning maths, I worked on my art, while he sat in a chair listening to a symphony concert and reading a book. My parents remained blissfully ignorant of the arrangement.

The War influenced every part of my young life. American air force troops were stationed in Snettisham, Norfolk, close to Sandringham, in the once brightly coloured beach huts that been adapted for wartime use. During the summer, I worked as a part time assistant in the local swimming pool, which was opposite the Kit Kat dance hall. The servicemen often came for a swim before crossing the road for drinks and dancing. The Americans were friendly to local people. I watched over their possessions when they were swimming and, in return, they brought me candy and gifts. They often shared the parcels of food and clothing that their families sent over, which was a great help during the rationing. Later, they adopted me as their mascot and I was given the honour of opening buildings within their camp. I often cycled the eight miles from Hunstanton to Snettisham, to where a road block had been set up at the entrance way to the camp. I gave my password and went freely into the camp, where I was taken in and spoilt by everyone.

When an invasion on Norfolk seemed imminent, I was asked by friends of my parents to join a local amateur dramatic company. We toured the county performing a play, which told people what to do if the German army arrived. My role was to walk onto the stage and announce that I was a secret resurgent and, if the German army occupied Norfolk, I would carry messages from village to village by bicycle. The plan was that hopefully the enemy wouldn't suspect my mission, as I was just a twelve-year-old boy. I enjoyed the stage life and being spoilt by the cast but the thought of what could have happened if I had completed this dangerous mission and been captured now turns me cold.

From the start of the War, people began to work hard to raise money for the war effort. Everyone was eager to do whatever he or she could to help. Money was scarce and many goods were rationed but we all did our bit. People knitted socks, jumpers, balaclavas, gloves and scarves for sailors in the Navy. Others organised concerts and performances. The soldiers stationed in our town gave their services by loaning us their army bands and various skills whenever an event was organised. Local people made cakes and sandwiches, which was a great sacrifice due to the rationing. Every farm was used in some way to raise money for the many charities and the needs of the services, the Red Cross and St John's Brigade.

Patricia and I, along with a cousin and other local children, organised ourselves into a determined team to raise money for local charities. We started by selling patriotic flags but soon developed more creative ideas and started to plan an ambitious performance. We persuaded an aunt to lend us her large garage. A local fireman built us a stage. We begged a piano from the nearby church, and convinced the greengrocer's daughter to play it, and began to rehearse our amateur show. I designed and made costumes from old clothes and materials given by friends and relations and made scenery and props from whatever I could find. I painted posters to advertise the show and persuaded shopkeepers to display them in their windows. The show was a great success and the garage was full of an audience of family and local people.

Spurred on by our achievements, Patricia and I decided to start another enterprise, this time making small gifts and hand-icrafts. During the War, many items were in short supply and it was difficult to buy interesting and original decorations in the shops. We saw a gap in the market and an opportunity to put our artistic skills to good use. Encouraged by my mother, who recognised our entrepreneurial flair, we spent all our spare time producing a range of toys and gifts. When she saw everything that we had produced, she let us sell our work on trestle tables outside her shop. This was a good catch for the soldiers, who were stationed in the large houses they used as barracks. We knew that they were always eager to find gifts for their families back home. On the day of the sale, we prayed for fine weather, set up our stall and covered it with flags and bunting. We had chosen a Thursday, early closing day, and the response was incredible. The soldiers bought toys for their children, towns-people bought gifts, and the raffle was drawn by a local celebrity. We were proud to hand all our takings over to the Prisoner of War Fund.

All these activities, combined with the pressure of up-coming exams at school and helping my mother in her shop, got the better of me and I became ill. The doctor recommended that I needed rest and recuperation and so I was sent to spend the summer on a fruit and poultry farm in the middle of nowhere. There I spent blissful days helping to feed the poultry, collecting the eggs, gathering the fruit and gleaning fallen corn from the harvest fields. The path from the house was lined on either side with Greengage trees so, whenever I went to collect the eggs or to feed the poultry, I was able to feast on delicious ripe fruit. Every night, I went to bed early, exhausted and happy.

When it was time for me to leave the farm, I was sent off with a small addition to my luggage – a crate containing a baby duckling. When I returned home, Patricia and I built a small pen in the garden on top of the air raid shelter that my father had built. I named the duckling Jackie and he soon became like a member of the family. He even joined us for walks and took advantage of a dip in the boating lake as we passed. This handsome bird deserved some company of his own kind and I realised that money could be made from my little feathered friend. I wrote to the farm and soon another crate arrived, this time containing five ducklings. This still wasn't enough for what I had planned, so I went to the market in King's Lynn and to a farm in Downham and bought ducks, bantams, a turkey and hens. I gradually took up more and more of our garden as I collected my stock and convinced several neighbours to allow me to use their gardens. I registered myself as a poultry breeder, collected scraps from local hotels and sold eggs to them in return. It was a very good start to my business life.

My artistic talents were well known in our small town and Marshalls, a glassware store on the High Street, approached me to make some gifts for them to sell. I set up a studio at the top of the house and worked like mad to fulfil the orders. I made fancy gifts out of anything I could lay my hands on, which was limited because of wartime shortages. I bought up a lot of cork table mats and painted them in bright patterns. I knitted toys, gloves and scarves. I decorated scallop shells and turned them into pin trays. I made wax jewellery and decorated glassware. Everything sold quickly, particularly to the summer trippers who flocked to the town. The money I earned from selling eggs paid for the materials and at last I was building up my capital. I quietly became a good businessman. I often wonder how I ever had the time to do my homework.

I was fifteen when the War finally ended and I decided to organise a bonfire party for the children of Hunstanton to celebrate our freedom. We had grown up during the War and had never enjoyed a Guy Fawkes celebration so I set about organising a night to remember. I convinced the soldiers living in the barracks opposite our house, who were waiting to be demobilised, to let me use their garden. Everyone brought pieces of wood and branches and a huge bonfire began to take shape. We had very few fireworks but the bonfire was magnificent. Once lit, it gave off such a heat that the people living nearby began throwing pails of water over their front doors to stop the paint blistering. When Guy Fawkes was finally placed on the summit, the blaze rivalled that of the Blitz. We roasted potatoes in the embers and when we finally left the garden in the early hours of the morning we were tired and dusty with ash but delighted.

The time was fast approaching for me to leave school and make a career for myself. I had no doubts about what I wanted to do and told the Headmaster firmly that I wanted to be a dress designer. My parents were consulted and agreed that, if that was what I really wanted, they would do all they could to help me. First, I had to pass all my art exams and the School Certificate. This was the motivation that I needed and for the first time I really settled down to my academic work. I dedicated myself to my school work for a year and slowly climbed up to the top position in my form. I sacrificed all pleasures and entertainments and took one exam after another and finally sat the dreaded School Certificate. Until I knew the results, I could not relax. I spent my summer anxiously waiting.

At last news came – I had passed. Now, I faced a new problem. All the art schools were crammed with service people on grants. When the War ended, men and women returned to civilian life and began to look for new training and jobs. Many enrolled on art courses and it was a great battle to get into the best art school. My parents were beginning to have doubts about the whole idea and it seemed that the dream was about to be snatched from my grasp. My art teacher believed in me and spurred me on. She spoke to my parents and convinced them that I had the necessary talent and gave me the addresses of several schools she thought suitable. I wrote letter after letter without success and eventually decided to use some of my savings to visit London and try the personal approach.

By July, I had a foot in the door. The Principal of the Chelsea School of Commercial Art gave me an interview. He said that they could take me on but, as it was a private art school, the fees were high. This did not discourage me and I wrote to the Norfolk Education Committee asking for funding and was granted an interview. I went to the head office in Norwich carefully dressed in my dark grey school suit and full of ambition to make beautiful clothes. I was told the grant I was seeking was equal to a university grant and asked how I was able to justify it. My reply simply was that I would succeed.

A few weeks later, a letter arrived to say that the grant had been awarded. Now everything was set. All I had to do was to find some accommodation in London. An aunt and uncle, who were also my godparents, lived in Putney, South West London, and offered me the use of two rooms, one for a bedroom and the other for an art studio, for a nominal rent. All I had to do was to wait until January 1948 to start at the art school in Chelsea. Then, I could at last begin my life in post-war London and make my long-awaited entry into the fashion world.

Chapter Four

Chelsea

On a cold January morning in 1948, I took an early bus to Chelsea. By the time I arrived at the studio at 50 Glebe Place, off the Kings Road, I was excited beyond words. I was seventeen years old, just a young man from Hunstanton, and this was the most incredible thing that had ever happened to me. I was about to take my first steps in London on my chosen career path and would soon be meeting all the other new students who were just as eager as me to begin their adventures.

The art school was a large studio with a minstrel gallery, open brick fireplaces and an inner courtyard. It was a place bubbling with creativity and dedication. It was full of hard working students who understood the opportunities that they were being given. We studied illustration under the tuition of Ian Hassall and Mr Johnston. Ian Hassall, whose father was a famous poster artist and whose brother worked alongside Ivor Novello, inspired and guided me from the beginning. Mme Pauline Rutter, who later became Mrs Stevenson, taught fashion drawing and design and was instrumental in encouraging my work. Other artists appeared on various days to give tuition. For me, it was the perfect place to be and I began to feel that I had at last found my place in the world.

The Director of Studies at the time was Bernard Adams, a strict man with little time for fashion. Instead, he tried to steer all his students towards the fine art section of the school, where I did not feel I belonged. Each week, students who had worked hard were invited to his studio on the Kings Road where we were shown the latest pictures he was preparing for upcoming exhibitions. He explained his techniques and served us China tea and éclairs. It soon became an unofficial challenge to see how many éclairs each set of students could eat.

I worked hard and soon became head student and with this honour came new responsibilities. It was my job to book models for life drawing classes and these included a then virtually unknown Quentin Crisp. He was an excellent model and could hold very difficult poses for long periods of time. Another of my tasks was to choose items from various antique shops in Chelsea for students to paint in still life classes. I roamed the shops choosing antique vases and lamps and soon developed an appreciation of antiques. Later, I was appointed as a steward to an antique exhibition in the little church in World's End, Chelsea. Queen Mary was the patron and, after she had reviewed the Guard of Honour, I was presented to her. I was in awe of her majestic appearance and her great knowledge of antiques.

Chelsea was very different from today's modern art school. It was a tightly run establishment and for many female students it was viewed almost as a finishing school where they could enjoy art while they did the Season. Young men were seeking a new life and career after the War and many enrolled in art colleges. It was still rare for men to work as fashion designers and instead they were more likely to be employed as window dressers and fashion artists. For everyone, art school was less about self expression, as it is now, and more about artistic appreciation. We studied many art forms and learned the technical skills of drawing and painting. We prepared ourselves to use art in a very practical way in our future careers.

There was quite a casual form of dress at Chelsea but nothing like you would find at an art school today. The boys wore sports jackets and flannels. The girls dressed well and in the late afternoons they accepted invitations to receptions and parties all over London. I always dressed formally, as I had done in Hunstanton, and each day arrived at Chelsea wearing a well-cut dark suit.

It was an awakening for me to finally be in London and to see all the fashions paraded before me on the city streets. There were still clothing rations and shortages but everyone was beginning to get back to the high standards they experienced before the War. This was clearly expressed by clothes they wore. Women dressed formally, despite the clothing rations, and always wore a hat, gloves, court shoes and stockings. They hungrily devoured pictures in magazines and newspapers and followed the new trends each season, adapting them depended on what they had available. When demobilised from the services, men were each given a suit, which they wore with a collar and tie for all occasions. It was the accessories that really made the outfit. Men working in the city wore bowler hats, carried gloves and an umbrella and some even wore red carnations as buttonholes in their dark city suits.

It was a time for creative dressing and making use of what you had available but at the same time following a strict sense of fashion. There were little tricks so that you always looked your best. Jewellery could be worn to instantly revive a tired outfit. Department stores, such as Liberty, launched a range of affordable headscarves, which helped to freshen up old clothes and gave the wearer a new look. People took pride in their appearance and clothes were a status symbol. Everyone wanted to look his or her best at all times.

Part of our artistic education was to find inspiration all around us and so went on trips all over London. We were sent to draw objects in the streets of Chelsea and at the Natural History Museum or the Victoria and Albert Museum in South Kensington. We were taken to couture shows in Mayfair fashion houses for previews of their collections. We drew everything that we could find.

One trip was to Bertram Mills Circus at Olympia, where we sketched the performers and animals as they prepared for the evening show. As far as I was concerned, there was far too much to see to limit myself to just drawing what I saw in front of me. I wanted to experience everything. I roamed about and talked to everyone and learned that later that morning a camera crew was going to start filming. I hung around excitedly and soon found myself involved in the shooting of a scene in a Just William film.

I can't remember how long I stayed with the circus folk but I do remember that I saw a dazzling evening performance from back stage. The next day, while most of the students had sketchbooks full of drawings, I had only my memories to offer. These were worth far more to me than any sketches.

We often went to the Natural History Museum to find subjects to draw but the visits soon turned into a regular social occasion. We arrived at the museum and drew our subjects as quickly as possible and then darted to the tearoom on the first floor, where they served the best cream cakes in the whole of London. The waitresses soon got to know us as we spent hours there, swapping gossip about the parties of the night before. We looked out of the window and kept watch over the people coming and going through the main door below. As soon as we saw the art master arriving to meet us, we finished our cakes and dash down the stairs. By the time he reached us, we were always grouped innocently round a case of stuffed birds, drawing like young Michelangelos.

At the end of each term, the college held a grand dance. The students chose a theme and the art studios were elaborately decorated. For one of these dances, we chose Montmartre as the theme and everyone came dressed as Apache dancers and bohemian artists. We began planning weeks ahead of the event and did all the decorating ourselves. At one end of the studio, we hung canvases painted with windows looking out from a cellar in Montmartre onto a view complete with cats and dustbins. The wooden stairs were disguised as iron ones and the scene was lit by candles in Chianti bottles.

One girl decided that there was a shortage of men at the party and invited the whole upper deck of a Liberty boat, which happened to be visiting the Pool of London. At 2am, we discovered that one of the sailors had passed out drunk in a corner. The Principal was at the party to keep a strict eye on us and it would be a disaster if the sailor was discovered. So, we quickly hid him in the bathroom. Unfortunately a girl came in and, mistaking the sailor for a corpse, began to scream. It was thanks to the noise of the band, and the general hubbub of the party in the main studio, that no one heard her cries and came running. The dance continued until the Principal decided to check the bathroom. He was furious when he found the sailor and ordered us to remove him from the premises immediately. We couldn't think what to do with him and, knowing that we couldn't leave him on the pavement, we put him into the back of a guest's car to sleep it off.

When the party was over, the car's owner offered to give some of the girls a lift home. They fitted themselves in round the sleeping sailor but, to their horror, another drunken guest jumped into the driving seat. The next hour was terrifying. Round and round the block they tore with the girls screaming out of every window and the sailor, now fully awake, trying to jump out. The police arrived on the scene. A crowd of us ran behind the car and begged the driver to stop, with the police following behind us. The procession made its way towards the river with everyone thinking that the end was near when suddenly the car stalled. The girls jumped out, terrified and in a state of collapse, and were followed by the sailor, who was by now completely sober.

At the end of one term, I met and fell in love with a very elegant mannequin called Billie. She was full of fun and looked just like the ever-elegant Lana Turner and I, like most young men, couldn't resist her blue eyes and blonde hair. We went together to our end of term dance and, when it was time to leave, balloons were released from the ceiling and we collected a large bunch. This was not enough for Billie who had spotted a pair of small decorated Christmas trees just inside the door. She begged me to get them for her as a keepsake and I, wanting to prove my gallantry to my new young lady, did as I was asked.

Carrying our mementoes between us, Billie with her bunch of balloons and I with a tree under each arm, we set off for the Kings Road. We hadn't got far when I felt a tap on my shoulder and turned round to see a policeman standing in front of me.

Amused at the sight of us, but deciding we had better not be left loose on the streets, he hailed a taxi and said, 'Now, you've both had a good evening and if I were you I would go straight home.'

We did as we were told but when we arrived at Billie's flat she realised that she had lost her key. She lived with her widowed mother and there was nothing for it but to ring the bell. It was 3am and a very sleepy mother opened the door. She was not at all pleased at being roused from her bed at this hour to find her daughter with a bunch of balloons and a strange young man carrying two decorated Christmas trees asking for a cup of coffee and a bed for the night.

I was having the time of my life at art school but I began to realise that it was fashion that really interested me. After one inspiring visit to the couture house of Mattli on Carlos Place, I knew where I wanted to be. I grew more and more restless and my frustration was soon spotted by Mme Rutter, the head of our fashion department. She suggested that I take some extra evening classes to speed up my training. She had just started to teach at St Martin's School of Art (later renamed Central Saint Martins College of Art and Design) and invited me to join. I studied there for two evenings a week and also undertook a course of pattern cutting under Mrs Swann, a teacher who made theatrical costumes in her own workrooms. I was desperate to progress in my training and so also began to study dressmaking and cutting in the evenings at Hammersmith College.

I began to spend every available minute drawing and studying fashion history but still had a nagging feeling of dissatisfaction, as though life wasn't moving fast enough. One evening after school, several of us went to a local pub for a drink and among the party was Mme Rutter. We talked and I tried to explain how unsettled I was feeling. Mme Rutter had some French friends in London who had hosted Christian Dior when he visited London as a student. She offered to speak to them to see if it would be possible for me to work in Paris under the great master. This was just the kind of opportunity that I needed. I worked night and day over the next few days to prepare a portfolio of designs and went with Mme Rutter to meet her friends. They were charming and complimented my designs and promised to write straight away to Dior in Paris.

The days that followed were among the most anxious in my

life. Eventually the answer came – Dior had promised to let me work for him but, because of restrictions of the French dress-making industry at the time, he could not pay me. I knew that I couldn't survive in a foreign city with no money and so had to turn down the offer. It was a terrible feeling and, once I had abandoned the idea, I began to fall into depression.

I needed a new plan to shake me out of my situation and to renew my excitement for fashion. Several days later, the telephone rang during lessons and Mme Rutter was called away. When she returned, she came to my desk and handed me a scrap of paper. On it was simply written an address, 'Lachasse, 4 Farm Street', a telephone number and a time. After school, she told me that she thought it was time I left Chelsea and gained some practical experience. She had spoken to Elizabeth Condy, a mannequin at Lachasse, who had spoken to Mr Todd, the head cutter and a Director of the company. It turned out that he was interested in bringing some young blood into the business. Here was my chance at last.

Chapter Five

Early Training

In November 1948, I arrived at Lachasse for my interview, clutching my drawings and some basic patterns that I had cut at evening classes. The first person I met was the head packer, Mr Heagerty, who showed me into the main showroom, a large, square room surrounded with mirrors. There was a large marble table and several gold settees were arranged round the walls. I was asked to wait while various people came and went, among them several women who each gave me a severe look. I felt like a goldfish in a bowl, simultaneously thrilled and terrified.

Elizabeth arrived and chatted animatedly to me until Mr Todd arrived to interview me. He asked me several questions, looked at my work and asked me seriously what I really wanted to do in the fashion trade and why I had chosen it as a career. I replied unhesitatingly that my ambition was to be a designer and that my family were not too keen on the idea. I assured him that I had definitely made up my mind that fashion was to be my future. Next came the question of National Service, which at that time all young men of my age had to do. I had been excused so far since I had not yet finished my education but once I left the Chelsea it would be a different matter. Mr Todd told me that there was no opening for a junior in the showroom but he could give me a full time job in his workroom. He took me upstairs and showed me through a glass door to the room, where I would work if I decided to join Lachasse.

I didn't know what to do and decided to wait until after Christmas to make up my mind. At the end of term, I went home to Norfolk and could think of nothing else but the job offer and my future. I was committed to stay at the Chelsea for three years and I had only completed one. I was now head student and had so far done very well with my studies. I had spoken to the Principals of the school and they had made it quite clear that they thought I needed some experience in the trade but that I should consider my options very carefully. The decision was mine to make. I turned this over and over in my mind and eventually decided that I must go back to London and talk to Mr Todd again. He was very honest and told me that he could promise nothing until I had learned some of the practical side of the trade and that whatever happened in the future would be up to me. I took a deep breath, made the decision that was to alter the course of my whole life, and accepted the job.

It was on a Monday morning in January 1949, two years after Christian Dior had changed the fashion world with the launch of the 'New Look', when I set off from my aunt and uncle's house in Putney to my first real job in fashion. When I arrived at Lachasse, I was shown upstairs to the workroom where I was to begin my career. There were several young men and women there already and they showed me to my place where I waited for my new teacher, Connie. Connie had been in the trade for about fifteen years and knew everything about making couture clothes. I discovered that, apart from being one of their best workers, she had wonderful patience for teaching young people. Before she arrived on that first morning, her junior came in – a small, dark haired girl who took very little notice of me and made it clear from the beginning that she did not like the look of me. Connie, luckily, came in smiling and organised herself for the day's work. By now the room had filled with tailors with their assistants. The whole room became a hive of activity.

I soon discovered that I had arrived on Rehearsal Day. There were to be endless rehearsals for the showing of the new collection and certainly very little time to teach me anything that day. I made endless cups of tea and did all kinds of odd jobs, mostly taking the tacks out of various pieces of fabric that had just been machined. I was beginning to feel that I was being useful but when I returned the first piece of fabric to Connie she looked at it in horror. In my eagerness, I had taking out all the vital balance marks as well as the tacks. I blushed as she told me to practise a variety of stitches on a piece of cloth.

By 4.30pm, all the garments were ready and we all went down to the showrooms to see the half-finished collection. This gave a designer the chance to change any major details and the staff could see what was still needed to be done to perfect their work. It was a wonderful show and I loved every second of it. I knew that this was something I would be happy to do every day. The main showing was just two days away and little did I realise how much work still had to be done in such a short time.

I could not do enough or do it quickly enough but gradually I learned that great love and care had to be put into every stitch. I was taught the correct way to make a garment from the first fitting to the final pressing and lining. I could soon make simple shapes and was filled with ambition to show my family what I could do. So, with the pieces of material left over from finished garments, I made skirts and little sleeveless boleros for my mother and sister. This helped me to learn about the cutting and fitting of clothes. I thought that I would need to stay in the work-rooms for about two years to learn all there was to know about clothes but I quickly discovered that I had considerably under-estimated the time it takes to learn this trade. People seldom realise exactly how much work goes into making these clothes. In fact, tailoring is much more like sculpture than most people imagine.

During 1952, whenever I wasn't working at Lachasse, much of my time was spent back stage at the Saville Theatre in Shaftesbury Avenue. After my evening art lessons at St Martin's School of Art, I crossed the road to the stage door of the Saville and entered a different world. I met the singer Adelaide Hall while she was appearing there in the musical 'Love from Judy' in a series of dazzling costumes. I watched the musical over and over but I never tired of it. Once back stage, I never knew who I might meet. It was in this show that Jean Carson first made her name and I soon found out that she was as charming off stage as she was in her role as the little orphan girl. June Whitfield was in the show as were Bill O'Connor, Johnny Brandon and Neil Arden. They were a talented bunch of youngsters and all went on to become household names. Backstage at the Saville was like a marvellous theatrical club and quite unlike my routine life in the workroom. It gave me inspiration for my work as I was surrounded by excitement and beautiful costumes.

One day without warning, my call-up papers arrived. As soon as I saw the envelope lying on the doormat, I knew that my life might change. I had always been under the doctor's care for my back deformity and he gave me a letter to take to the medical board. I took the day off and went to Kingston-on-Thames where I joined dozens of other boys awaiting their fate.

I was asked which service I wanted to join and replied, 'the Royal Air Force.'

With a dozen other young men, I was shown into a separate room and given an interview. We waited for about half an hour for our results and I was told that I was among those who could join the Air Force, with the remainder of the men going into the Army. Now, came the medical examination and we were passed from doctor to doctor, who each poked and prodded and asked questions. Once this ordeal was over, we were allowed to go home to await the final results. About ten days later, I received another letter. This time it was a little fawn card marked Grade III, which meant that I was not fit enough for the forces and could continue my career unhindered.

Realising how lucky I was, I threw myself back into my work. I had a full timetable of work at Lachasse during the day and then evening classes at St Martin's School of Art. I still ran my own business making fancy goods and sold them to the shop in Norfolk and had been given a contract to supply a shop in Putney. Sometimes, I worked eighteen hours a day and, not surprisingly, I found my health suffering again. I tried giving up some of my evening classes but I developed into a robot and could not keep still for a second. If one evening I decided to stay at home and rest, I always found myself staying later at Lachasse, working on clothes for my family. There was always something to do in London and when I wasn't at work I was constantly out at exhibitions, concerts and shows.

I had been working at Lachasse for two years when my colleague Connie was taken ill and it was decided that I should now take on my own work. This was a big responsibility and I was trusted to do some of the jobs on difficult garments such as coats and boleros. After six months on my own, I was given a junior to teach and four months later I was given a second junior. All this was good experience for me but it meant that in order to keep the two juniors working at full speed I also had to work equally hard and my health began to suffer.

When I went home to Norfolk for a weekend, I was completely worn out and my family hardly recognised me. The family doctor saw me immediately and ordered me to stay at home for a complete rest. This seemed unthinkable. I had so much work to do and so much left to learn. Lachasse were very kind and assured me that, however long my rest needed to be, my job would be waiting for me when I returned. I was desperate to get back to London but soon relaxed back into my old life by the sea. The rest, which I had hoped would take only a few weeks, took eight months. I left Norfolk and returned to London with some stern advice from my doctor about how much work I was able to take on.

While resting in Norfolk, I had begun to realise the direction I wanted my career to take. I now knew that I wanted to learn as much as possible about cutting, fitting and making clothes. I knew that I needed to widen my experience of the industry and thought I should try to find a new job. So, after making a long list of addresses of suitable employers, I wrote to each one. I went to several interviews and looked around famous couture houses, such as John Cavanagh, Victor Stiebel, Hardy Amies and Ronald Patterson. I tried contacting wholesale houses but, since I only had experience of working at the couture end of the trade, my ideas and designs were far too extravagant for the ready-to-wear market. Every time the negative answer came from a prospective employer my heart sank a little deeper.

My first break came when I saw an advertisement for a firm

on Bruton Street who were looking to buy new designs. I took them a selection of sketches, which I showed to the designer and cutter, and they bought some of my designs. My relationship with them continued and I regularly showed them my designs and they picked out what they liked. Then, a toile was made for me to go to see during my lunch break from Lachasse. I then made suggestions and adjustments until the finished garment looked just as I had imagined.

Inspired by my success, I longed to do more work of this kind. A few months later, I saw an advert in a national paper looking for freelance dress designers. I rang the telephone number straight away. The voice that answered was quite unlike anything I had ever come across in the fashion trade. She sounded just like a cockney parrot. She told me that it was her son who was in the wholesale fashion business and asked me to ring back later. This I did and found that his voice was marginally less raucous than that of his mother. We agreed to meet at what he said was his club and, since I had not had much experience of clubs in Soho, it sounded in order to me. I arrived at the club with my sketches under my arm but, when I tried to enter, the doorkeeper barred my way and told me that entry was for members only. He did not believe that I had been asked to meet a member there. I was worried that I would miss my appointment and the opportunity that I was sure it would bring.

I waited outside and eventually a man came along and asked me if I wanted to go into the club. At once I said yes and he agreed to take me in as his guest. Immediately inside the door, as a steep staircase descended into the nether regions lit by the dimmest possible light, I was seized with fear. I climbed down and, on reaching the bottom, saw several men drinking at a bar. The style of the décor confirmed my worst suspicions but nevertheless I asked the attendant if he could point out the man with whom I had an appointment. I was directed to another, if anything sleazier, area of the club and was eventually met by a small, quite neatly dressed man. I sat and showed him my work, which he said he liked very much. He was in partnership with his sister and asked if I would call on them again the following

Monday so that she could also see my designs. I agreed and beat a hasty retreat.

Having gone so far, I decided I had better go through with it. So on Monday, I went back to Soho with my sketches. I searched for the address I had been given and was about to give up when I spotted a sign over a third floor window. Up I went and knocked on the door but once inside there was no sign of the sister. The man told me that she was ill and he asked me to leave the designs for her to look at and return to collect them the next day.

I fell for this, not having been warned about the traps of the fashion trade, and left the sketches. When I returned the next day quite the most ruthless-looking woman I had ever seen opened the door and invited me to come in and wait for her brother. I sat in a bare, empty room for about forty minutes, conscious that my lunch break was only three quarters of an hour long, until eventually the man arrived. He spoke to his sister, showed her some papers and completely ignored me until I stood up and said I had to leave and needed my sketches back. At this, he handed me my book of designs, saying that they were quite unsuitable for his needs. I was enraged at the treatment and left in a hurry to get back to Lachasse. A few weeks later, I was amazed to see some of my designs made up in a small shop in Soho, exact to the last detail. I learned a valuable lesson about the other side of the fashion trade, one that can only be learned by experience.

Still restless and looking for new opportunities, I did all I could to sell my own work. By now the training period of those people who had left the services and gone into the art schools had just finished and the trade was flooded with would-be dress designers and fashion artists. It was hard to find work anywhere within the fashion industry. It was getting more and more difficult for me to me follow my dreams. I still wasn't quite sure of my place in fashion but I was ambitious and wanted a new challenge.

Chapter Six

My Danish Friend

When visiting St Martin's School of Art one evening, I was asked to help a young Danish student who had got into difficulties with sewing a garment for an exam. He was putting in a gusset for some Magyar sleeves and had reached an unmanageable point, which occasionally happens to all students. We had several garments with Magyar sleeves in the current collection at Lachasse and so I was happy to help. This was how I met Ola Norring. He had a great zest for life and was always racing around London full of great ideas. He lived in a small hotel in Hampstead and worked to supplement the allowance his father sent him each week. We quickly became friends and often met for Sunday lunch, followed by a walk in the beautiful grounds of Kenwood House.

One Sunday, I arrived to find Ola in a very nervous state. He had taken an order to make a full-length winter topcoat made from gold monkey-hair fabric and had forgotten for a moment that he knew very little about tailoring. He had agreed to make the coat and needed the money but had no idea how to complete the commission. Things had already gone very wrong but, determined as he was, he carried on and hoped for the best.

His sister Dorothy, a fashion mannequin in London, made us tea and cake and I started to help Ola get ready for the fitting. I am not quite sure what the nationality of the client was, or her profession, but when Ola put the coat on her there was a great deal of serious talking in her language and in Ola's Danish. I gathered from his gestures that he was trying to reassure her that all would be well. The coat was hanging in the most extraordinary way and had the oddest pair of sleeves that I had ever seen. Ola continued to pin and push the atrocious-looking material into his idea of what it should look like. He knelt on the floor and with a worn-out tape measure proceeded to put a few pins into the hem. Then, he took a large pair of cutting shears and began to cut the fabric off the bottom. I looked on in amazement as, starting from left to right, he cut right round the coat. The inevitable happened and when he reached his starting point the two lengths were still as uneven as before. As I struggled to stop laughing, the client became increasingly restless.

Ola tried again with the tape measure, the pins and the shears and again the two edges were just as uneven as before. The coat was getting shorter and shorter and was soon a seven-eights-length coat. There was more talking and hand waving with the client and round he went again. Now, it was definitely a three-quarter-length coat. At this, his client called a halt and a long discussion took place. To my surprise, she eventually settled for a coat that just topped the hip line. After she left, I couldn't contain myself any longer and laughed until I cried.

Ola was not at all amused and said firmly, 'Well, it was a ghastly colour and fabric, and I just told her the less she wore of it the better for everyone!'

The poor woman had paid in advance for the coat and had very little choice once the fabric had been cut off.

One day when I met Ola, he was full of excitement. He had been asking me to meet a very famous friend of his for weeks and had at last been able to arrange a meeting. He refused to say who it was but told me to meet him at Jules Bar on Jermyn Street the next day at 6.30pm. Wondering just who this famous person was, I waited eagerly for their arrival. Ola arrived alone and I began to think that this was his idea of a joke. We had a drink together and waited. Eventually, the door opened and in walked a dapper fair-haired man wearing a large bow tie. It was Aage Thaarup, the royal milliner. With him were his head milliner Elizabeth Voss and his sister and brother-in-law, who were visiting London from Denmark.

It was obvious that the evening was going to be a memorable

one. After we had got to know one another over drinks, we set out for a tour of London by car and then on to dine at a small restaurant in Soho. I soon learned that Aage didn't just make wonderful hats; he also knew where to find the best food in London. I think I learned more about London that evening than I had ever known before. When we parted, I was given a firm promise that I could view Aage's new collection at his premises. It was a wonderful opportunity for me at this early stage in my career.

Several weeks later, Aage Tharrup contacted Ola with some exciting news. Some of his business friends were leaving their Park Lane flat to go to the South of France on holiday and he had arranged for Ola to stay there for the whole time they were away. All he had to do in exchange was look after their two Siamese cats. He asked me to join him and it sounded like a wonderful opportunity for two young men to live in the heart of the West End for three weeks in perfect luxury. It was easy to get used to living in the centre of London. We popped home at lunchtime and help ourselves to food from the well-stocked fridge. On Saturdays, we went shopping and then to Fortnum & Mason for coffee. We both bought bowler hats from Locks and I wore a Carnation in my button hole each day. We were living the life of wealthy gentlemen.

The end of our three-week holiday in Mayfair came all too soon and we decided to throw a party. Ola wrote to his family in Copenhagen to ask them to send some food parcels and these arrived full of appetizing tins of ham and other cooked meats. My aunt had taken a course at the Marshall School of Cookery so we begged her to make cocktail snacks. We sent out the invitations and our original list of twenty guests grew into a much larger one. We thought that we had only chosen those people who were safe to have in our borrowed flat but when we added up the list it had grown to seventy-five.

I set to work making a list of all the jobs that needed to be done but I couldn't plan for everything. The day before the party, my sister phoned to say that our mother had fallen and injured her wrist while out shopping. She was very upset and asked me to go straight back to Hunstanton. I left for home, giving Ola a list of strict orders to follow and a promise that I would be back soon. I wanted everything to be perfect for the party and I definitely wasn't going to miss it for anything.

Fortunately, when I got home my mother's arm had been x-rayed and it was not as bad as it had first appeared. I went back to London and arrived an hour before the guests were due to arrive to find Ola doing a little of each job but finishing nothing. I decided that the best thing to do was to organise the room in which the party was to be held. Then we remembered the cats. They were highly-strung and nervous of strangers. We couldn't leave them with all the guests so we tried to shut them in the bedroom. What we didn't realise was that we had left the bedroom windows open. Moments later, here was a knock at the door and a red-faced porter informed us that both cats were clinging to the window ledge outside and a crowd was gathering in the street below. He warned us that the Fire Brigade or the Police would have to be called if we could not retrieve the cats quickly. We coaxed and shouted but, despite all our efforts, the cats did not budge. We realised that we had to think like a cat and put a piece of cloth on a string and dragged it slowly across the ledge. This worked and one by one the cats were safely locked in the bedroom and the window was firmly closed.

The guests began to arrive. I left Ola to greet them and pour the drinks while I shut myself in the kitchen to finish the other preparations. I soon joined the party and, the moment I entered the room, I realised that we were in for a memorable evening. The guests came from a wide range of backgrounds but they all seemed to be mixing extremely well. The atmosphere was helped by Ola's intoxicating new cocktail recipe. The food rapidly disappeared and the drink was running out fast but it was obvious that people were enjoying themselves far too much to think of leaving. We turned on the music and the mass of guests began to shuffle about.

Then there was a flash. A press photographer from a gossip magazine had mixed with the crowd and was now taking shots of our friends enjoying themselves. Ola and I decided that drink was the only answer and we gave the man a large Pimms. Fortunately, it was not his first that evening and each time he took a picture we handed him another drink, until he became quite helpless and we were able to confiscate his camera. After this incident, I decided that we had quite enough of the eventful party and gradually the guests began to leave. The next morning, we cleared up and left the flat quietly after enjoying our period of luxurious living. Ola went back to Hampstead and I returned to the peace and calm of Putney.

Chapter Seven

First Clients

It was a few days before I saw Ola again but a telephone message asking me to meet him urgently at the Coffee Inn on Park Lane told me that something was on his mind. When I arrived, he said that Elizabeth Voss, head milliner for Aage Tharrup, had asked Ola if I would make her a silk suit. He had at once agreed and so I had no choice. I was terrified. I had never made any clothes for anyone outside my immediate family and certainly had not done much cutting. I could see that there was no way out and I was forced to agree. Elizabeth was to be my first real client.

It was the end of the season, when the large textile houses held their sales, so I arranged for Ola and me to buy the material. I then planned to cut it and Elizabeth would not see it until her fitting. I was taking a risk and my taste and judgement needed to be impeccable. My real problem was that I still had little experience of cutting. My colleagues at Lachasse gave me advice on how to take the measurements and guidance on how much material I was going to need.

Ola and I went to Frank Loynes, the first time I had been to a wholesale textile house. I was overwhelmed by mountains of beautiful fabrics in every colour and cloth imaginable and eventually chose a blue-green slub silk, which I thought would suit the Danish girl's fair complexion. I worked hard on the suit, from the cutting to the fitting and the finishing touches, and delivered it with great pride. Elizabeth planned to wear it at a cocktail party given by Lady Lumley Smith. About three weeks later, Ola gave me a message from Elizabeth telling me how pleased she was and how much her friends had admired her suit. Lady Lumley Smith liked it so much that she asked whether I could make her one too.

I was hesitant because I had not finished my training but before I had a chance to say no, Ola said firmly, 'You must. I have told Elizabeth you will.'

He had big plans for me and added, 'This will help you and one day you will have enough clients to open a fashion house of your own.'

I was very nervous, my hands were almost shaking as I cut the fabric, but I pretended to be calm and capable in front of my new client. Now, I had two clients of my own and both promised to place more orders.

Lady Lumley Smith often travelled with her husband and, just before one of these trips, she phoned me to ask if I could show her some of my own sketches as she wanted to place a large order. This was my first chance to try to make some of my own designs and to experiment with using different colours. It was an exciting opportunity for a young designer and I couldn't refuse. When I arrived at her house in Egerton Terrace, she told me that she needed various ensembles, including evening clothes. I took the job and it wasn't later until I realised just how much work it was going to be. I selected suitable sketches, chose materials and made patterns and worked every spare minute I could find until I delivered the finished clothes. I was beginning to feel like a real designer.

Once I had established one or two clients, others quickly followed. As my client list steadily grew, I was meeting a constant stream of people and my social network expanded. I was invited to endless parties and became quite well known in West End Society. My reputation spread across London and it was not long before I had every single second booked with work and I had to refuse orders. I often worked for eighteen hours a day. I spent the day working at Lachasse, lunchtime searching for fabric for clients and the evening working on their orders. I was learning rapidly through trial and error and experimented with new techniques. I began to understand how to design for all kinds of figures and the art of manipulating materials to help to flatter a woman. I became fascinated by colours and textures and looked for inspiration for my designs everywhere I went. I recorded everything in my sketchbook, a habit that I had picked up while studying at Chelsea.

Despite all my hard work, I still felt there was more I could do. The familiar sense of dissatisfaction was returning and I longed for a new challenge. My dream was always open to a fashion house of my own but this was beyond my reach as I felt I could never find enough capital. I began to look round for other opportunities.

At about this time, a mannequin called Virginia, who worked at Lachasse, introduced me to an acquaintance of hers. He was a young man who believed he was about to set the world of fashion on fire. Virginia invited me to have a drink with him and I accepted, since I was always ready to meet new and interesting people. We arrived at the mews house he shared with a friend and his butler showed us into a well-decorated sitting room. The door opened and in came a good-looking young man of about twenty. He offered us drinks and began talking. He had a grand plan to launch his own fashion house and he was looking for people to help. He was a mysterious man and hinted that he had someone in his background who was prepared to give him unlimited financial backing. It all sounded too good to be true but to each of my questions he had a ready and believable reply. I was slowly convinced that this was a genuine opportunity.

He proposed that I should be responsible for the practical side of the business and manage the workrooms, organise the fittings and help him get the collection ready. He showed me his own designs, which I thought were original and quite promising. I tried to be practical and not get carried away with the dream and so asked him about salaries. He asked me to make a list of the staff that I would need and their salaries and asked me what I would expect to be paid. It would be a huge job so I mentioned a sizeable sum. He wasn't shaken by the sum and turned to Virginia to discuss her role. She would be expected to help him run the showroom, model, answer the telephone and help sell the clothes. When asked what payments she would expect, she, like me, pushed up her price. Again, he did not seem put-out and we left on the understanding that when he had finalised his plans he would contact us. He had many ideas but, as yet, no premises and so needed to start looking straight away.

Virginia and I left, stunned by the whole idea. We went to a coffee house to talk things over and realised that we had dozens of questions that we had forgotten to ask the rather overpowering young man. Our main worry was that he hadn't discussed where he would find the clientèle. My own client numbers were growing steadily and I knew that I could rely on several friends to buy their clothes from me. Virginia had quite an influence in the fashion world and would do all she could to help but I knew it needed more than this. We were starting to get worried.

It was not long before we were invited to the mews house for a second time and there we were introduced to a woman of very little charm but obviously a great deal of power. It was clear that she was to be the head of it all and I took an instant dislike to her and her abrupt manner. The business was going to be funded by a shipping magnate friend of hers and she would be firmly in control. I had never met a woman who talked so much and who I distrusted so instantly. By the time we left, we had both agreed to join them but our minds were a whirl of unanswered questions.

The next day, Virginia and I met early to talk things over. We realised that there were far too many questions and not enough promise. We needed to get out of the plan, and quickly. We decided that we would say outright that it all sounded too shaky but, before we could contact the young man, he sent us an invitation to a cocktail party. We decided to go. We knew very little about him and began to wonder whether we had judged him too harshly. If we could see his friends we thought we would have enough information to make our final decision. So we arrived at the party and were shown upstairs and left in a room on our own. We could hear voices and the sound of glasses and laughter from another room.

When eventually our host appeared, he said how pleased he

History of Lachasse

F. W. Shingleton, Founder

Eva Gray, Mrs. Fred Shingleton

Berkeley Square 1930

Berkeley Square 1930

Back of Berkeley Square

4 Farmer Street, Berkeley Square

Schooldays and Burgeoning Creativity

Grandmother Lily Nelson
and Aunt Annie, Hurst House.

1947 King Edward VII

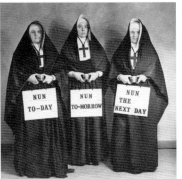

Mother and two friends
wearing costumes created
by PLC aged 16

1947 Guy Fawkes Bonfire

Boyhood

Age 3 years

Parents

1934

1935

With brother Richard and sister Patricia

The Mannequins

Virginia with a doll of herself scaled to 1/10th of the human body.
(Doll at The Fashion Museum, Bath) © *Mirrorpic*

Katy, for a convention of ensembles.
His and Hers outfits. © *Reuters*

From Sketch to Fitting

ED 34

From Sketch to Fitting

Special Collections

PLC giving a lecture at Oxford University

Evening Ensemble
© *John Cole at Studio Five*

The Top Ten Couture House Joint Fashion Show   © *Herbert de Gray*

Special Clients and Special Creations by PLC

HRH Marina, Duchess of Kent

The Countess of Lindsay

Mrs Alan McEwan

The boyhood dream come true – with Sheena

was to see us, gave us a stiff drink and said he had a surprise in store. He led us into another room, which was filled to capacity with people enjoying themselves. Immediately, he called for silence, led us to the centre of the room and announced in a loud voice that he was opening a fashion house in three months' time and introduced Virginia and I to the crowd. Camera flash bulbs popped and people began to wish us luck. I can't remember what I felt like or what Virginia looked like at that moment. I can only recall feeling very sick and seeing dizzying masses of white flashes. When we eventually came to our senses, I whispered that we must get away. This was quite easily done for, in all the excitement, our host had forgotten us while he gave interviews to the press.

Once out in the mews, we began to realise how dangerous any press coverage could be on our careers. Everything had moved so quickly that neither of us had told Lachasse about our plans to leave and so we were sure that we were both going to be out of jobs by the next day. As by now we didn't have the slightest intention of working for the young man, this would be a disaster. We walked for hours, wondering how we could get out of it all and keep our jobs at Lachasse. That night I could not sleep. On the bus the next morning, I craned over peoples' shoulders to see if I could catch a glimpse of a headline or a picture in any papers. As soon as I got to Lachasse, I slunk into my workroom and begged the girls to lend me their newspapers. To my relief, I couldn't find any mention of the launch of the new fashion house. When Virginia arrived at work, after also suffering a sleepless night, she told me that she had found the same thing. There was no mention of the news anywhere. We decided to visit the young man at lunchtime and let him know exactly where we stood. We definitely didn't want to be involved.

Virginia phoned him. He was out but we arranged a lunchtime meeting and raced round to the mews on our lunch break. The young man answered the door and he looked very much worse for wear. He ushered us in and gave us a drink and, before we could open our mouths, he blurted out that the whole thing was off. The oil magnate had never definitely agreed to finance him in the first place and, after hearing about the launch at the party the night before, he had threatened to sue the young man if the story got into the press. So, our host had spent the night begging his Fleet Street friends not to use the story, which a few hours earlier he had begged them to report. By the time Virginia and I left, we agreed not to take any more risks with fashion houses and to be content with our jobs at Lachasse. I was still impatient for new experiences and exciting opportunities but for now would try to find these in the job I already had.

A few months later, I realised that this plan was working as I was given the responsibility of cutting, fitting and making clothes for the new collection. Slowly, I was able to build up my own workroom and start training a few girls according to my own high standards. I loved this job. I was able to meet people from all walks of life in the fitting room and I began to realise what I really wanted to do. Miss Joyce, the managing Director of Lachasse, had the idea of introducing me to the clients by allowing me to help seat them at shows. This was more of a challenge than I expected and I soon adopted a technique that was worthy of a diplomat. It was a real challenge to get people to sit in the right seats at the right time and keep everything running smoothly. Having been seen working on show days at Lachasse, I was asked to help whenever we held a charity fashion show in other venues. This new responsibility took me to country houses across Britain and I met more and more people, who all had stories to tell about their lives.

On the day of one of our bi-annual fashion shows, I had just finished seating most of the clients when I found myself standing on the doorstep with the Miss Joyce. She suggested that I take a walk with her around the block, which immediately made me feel very nervous. As we walked, she asked me about my plans for my career. Then, completely unexpectedly, she offered me the post of *vendeur*, or salesman, in the showroom. She had apparently been watching me and had been trying me out for the post, which was soon to be vacated with the retirement of a very talented and popular *vendeuse*, or saleswoman.

Lachasse's showroom was dominated by four *vendeuse*. They

were all great characters, each with large lists of clients. Their word was law and they knew all the most intimate details about them. Their knowledge of style, colour and material was beyond belief and each of their clients relied on them for their honest advice. They earned small salaries but made up for it with commission on each sale. When their turnover reached £30,000, they were paid double commission. This arrangement kept everyone keen to look after their clients and to work hard to attract new ones. If the showroom was ever empty, everyone became quite desperate to attract trade. I wasn't sure if I was ready to join these women in this new role.

I was again faced with a difficult decision. I had planned that when I was ready to make a move and open my own fashion house it would be with the support of the Director. She had shown great interest in my career and kept my workroom going with her clients. She needed a decision straight away. I trusted her judgement and she thought that I would make a good *vendeur*. I listened to my heart and said yes. This was an excellent promotion and it was a job that I knew I would love.

It was decided that I would join the showroom staff in a few weeks, after I had finished any outstanding work and transferred my clients. It was customary for a *vendeuse* to give a season's notice so that she could be replaced by someone with the same qualifications. She suggested that she could train me and then transfer her clientèle to me. I agreed but as soon as we began my training, I realised that her standards were very high and the next few months were some of the hardest I have ever worked through. At some stages, I felt as though I would never make the grade. I realised that it was one thing to sell clothes after a fashion show but quite a different thing to take full responsibility on my own. I gradually began to learn lessons that were invaluable in my career in the showroom. The most important was the realisation that the client must always come first. When visiting Lachasse, every client should be made to feel as though she was our most important customer. I often had to persuade a woman that the gown she had seen in the collection, and had visualised herself wearing, was actually unflattering to her figure. I learned that a bad sale is a client lost and that sometimes the job took tact as well as skill.

By the time the season was over and I was firmly established in my new position, a new challenge presented itself to me and I was about to be busier than ever. I received a phone call from Muriel Remberton, the head of the fashion department at St Martin's School of Art, asking me to teach evening classes. Of course, I agreed. The following week, I arrived and took up my new post. As I entered the room, my throat turned dry and I could scarcely get a word out. By the time term ended, I longed for more. I was in the unique position of being able to work on the latest fashions all day and then pass on this knowledge to my students in the evening. Being at the school also meant that I was continually developing my fitting and cutting skills as well as improving my knowledge of the history of costume. This in turn helped me with my job during the day. The two jobs complimented each other perfectly and it seemed an ideal arrangement.

Over each year, I taught several hundred young men and women. Some, like Benny Ong, Bruce Oldfield, Rifat Ozbeck, John Galliano and Bill Gibb later found fame in the fashion world. Others made names in all branches of the trade, including fashion drawing and journalism and held down responsible jobs around the world.

While I found teaching rewarding, I sometimes felt frustrated by the lack of drive in many of the students I taught. It became increasingly obvious that many of them expected to leave college after three years training and receive salaries far above their actual worth. It was very difficult for me to explain to them that, in order to reach the top of their chosen profession, they had to work extremely hard and devote their life to their ambitions.

I was often amazed by the way the students dressed. They spent all day studying how to make beautiful clothes but their own clothing did not reflect this. At one time, I was shocked by the vogue among young male art students to look as much like Chicago gangsters as possible, with long, lank hair, tight jeans, black leather jackets and jack boots. During the '80s, I was amazed by the outfits of many of my female students. They had the most fantastic bouffant hair-dos, thick eye make-up, green nail varnish and the oddest of clothes. The vogue then was for black woollen leg warmers, white high heel shoes, very short skirts and jumpers full of holes. The effect was both startling and stunning. I always found, however, that it was the students who always dressed neatly and with the utmost care who I later read about in the fashion columns of the glossy magazines.

Chapter Eight

The Collection

Few people understand exactly how a collection is created and how it grows from the smallest idea into reality. Only someone working in close contact with a fashion designer can put into words the real feelings and hard work that go into building a collection. As I spent more time in the fashion industry, working at Lachasse, dressing my own clients and teaching the practical aspects of design, I began to understand it for myself.

Fashion in the couture trade was always quite different from the collections shown by some of the larger stores at their fashion shows. Couture houses, like Lachasse, set a new line each season and it was always original and often extreme. It had to be dramatic otherwise it would not be able to stand the watering-down process it goes through when it was sold to mass-market buyers.

At Lachasse, a new collection always started with the fabric. At the end of October, for the spring collection, and the beginning of March, for the winter collection, textile houses were asked to bring in their new fabric ranges to the studio for the designer to see. This was a huge task. Everyone, from the designers to the stock keepers, was kept busy with dozens of appointments each day. Every single piece of fabric brought to Lachasse was examined and every detail about texture and colour was noted. Day by day, the list of possibilities grew. There were so many people whose opinion needed to be heard. The designer wanted to find the perfect fabric from which to make beautiful clothes. The sales staff had knowledge about current trends and knew what would sell the next season. They each had their own clients and knew what they would want to buy. Lachasse was full of chatter, disagreements and excitement.

Each Lachasse collection contained thirty suits, twelve topcoats, blouses, cocktail wear and evening gowns, town and country clothes. After two days of sorting out materials, the designer began the slow process of deciding on the required number of patterns. These were left on the large table in the centre of the workroom with the designer walking around them until he found inspiration. Material was everywhere, draped over every available surface. It lay draped in piles to test if certain colours worked well together. It was hung up to see how a particular gown would look when worn. Slowly, the ideas for the collection emerged.

Once everything was chosen, the colours and yardages decided and the unwanted patterns returned, we began to choose mannequins to model the collection. For days, the showroom was full of women walking up and down in front of the designer as he constantly shook his head and only occasionally nodded. He may have seen a mannequin at a show and invited her to come and see him but then realised that she wasn't suitable to model his clothes. Slowly, eight girls were picked. Three were house girls employed to work throughout the season at Lachasse modelling clothes for clients. Five were freelance girls to model for the press shows, for overseas buyers and for fashion shows organised for clients. It was important that all the mannequins had similar measurements, so that each could model the whole collection.

Then the designer, along with his fashion artist, left Lachasse for a month to work in his own private studio. Here the designs were put on paper and gradually the collection took shape. From time to time, the sketches were shown to the Director or the Chairman. It was not until the whole collection had been put on paper that the designer returned to Lachasse.

We didn't just wait for his return, we were busy too. The fabrics began to arrive from textile houses all over the world. We were busy on the phone chasing lost orders and sorting out all the little and infuriating problems that arose. We were very protective of the fabric and kept the full range hidden until the collection had been launched. We didn't want anything to be misplaced and we certainly didn't want the sales staff taking orders on materials that we planned to keep on our secret list.

When the designer had finished all his sketches, they were brought in to Lachasse and shown to the sales staff, who gave their honest, and often brutal, reactions. This was a difficult time in the workrooms as everyone had an opinion and wanted it to be heard. Then, materials and sketches were given to each fitter. Each workroom specialised in a different type of garment. Some fitters preferred working with softer fabrics and some preferred the thicker, more tailored, type of cloth. It would be a disaster if the wrong style and fabric fell into the hands of the wrong fitter. Now, the battle really began. The sales staff needed the workrooms to make items from the current collection for their clients and the designer wanted the workrooms and fitters for his new collection. There was always a fight for space and we each had to work separately and at different times of the day.

Once the collection was finished, we had three rehearsals to prepare for the public launch, held in Lachasse's showroom. At the first rehearsal, all the mannequins were called in, along with the designer, milliner and sales staff, for a run through to check that the collection was ready. This rehearsal usually ended in heated arguments as everyone fought over everything, even down to the number of pleats on a suit. One person might say there were too many, someone else would think it was just right and the poor designer would be torn to pieces in the middle. Even the mannequins fought between themselves over what they would wear. Quite often, a suit or dress made for Virginia to wear was tried on Sally and for some unknown reason suited her better. This was where the most fierce arguments started. Virginia probably liked her dress and thought it looked better on her than on Sally. The designer and Director had to demonstrate great skill in persuading Virginia that she looked equally good in the other dress.

This first rehearsal often stretched long into the night and the next day it started all over again. The milliner and belt maker worked to add their finishing flourishes to the collection and, just before the second rehearsal, the hats and belts arrived along with the shoes. The furrier and jeweller were invited to the second rehearsal and they took notes and discussed what furs and jewels would be right for each ensemble. The hats were shown with the clothes and the battle began again. Everyone had an opinion. The fitter always took every comment as a personal attack and defended his or her garment. Every season, it was the same battle and, every season, the battle ended in peace.

The day after the second rehearsal, the designer chose the buttons, trimmings and all the finishing touches needed to complete his collection. When the clothes were almost ready all we had to do was wait for the late arrival of something or other. There were always last minute details to change and arrange.

The third and final rehearsal was almost like the real show. Everyone who contributed to the collection was invited and so the textile manufacturers, shoe suppliers, hairdressers, jewellers, furriers and artificial flower makers all arrived and took their seats to see the collection. The staff and mannequins were each allowed to invite one or two friends and this helped create the atmosphere of a real show.

At this rehearsal, the designer timed the mannequins and made notes of anything he felt needed adjusting. He might have suddenly taken a dislike to a belt or hat and this rehearsal gave him the last opportunity to have it altered. It also gave him a chance to see the reactions of different people to his new line and the mannequins could get a feel for the clothes they would soon be showing. After the final rehearsal, the collection was sent back to the workrooms for the final pressing and finishing off, ready for the first real show the next day. This first show was always for the press so that they could interpret the new trends for their readers.

On the morning of the show, all the staff arrived early and there was always a sense of excitement and tension in the air. Our famous gold chairs arrived to be arranged according to a careful seating plan. Beautiful flowers in large vases. Programmes were laid out on each chair. The dressing room was prepared with a clothes rack for each mannequin, full of the ensembles she was to wear and a list detailing the precise timings of the show. The mannequins arrived just as the designer began to get impatient.

Soon, he was shouting instructions to each girl, 'Cynthia dear, don't forget to show your black coat. Betty, make the most of your evening dress.'

From each girl, there came a disinterested grunt. Cynthia and Betty would be too busy putting on their false eyelashes and applying makeup to carry on a conversation.

The Director then arrived and gave each girl her quota of stockings, followed by a drink. This was a tradition partly to launch the collection and also to give the mannequins a final boost of confidence, in case they were suffering from stage fright. Then, after a quick inspection of each ensemble by the designer, the mannequins were ready to go. The signal was given, the lights went down, the spotlights went on and the show began. The first mannequin walked slowly across the room. Backwards and forwards she glided, with small slow steps, as she showed her ensemble to the eager audience. She was followed by the next mannequin and on, until the whole collection had been shown.

Once the press show was over, there was always a mad rush for the telephone and the door and a wild chatter of people seeking information about this or that garment. When the frantic activity had subsided, the photographers moved in. Each photographer handed me a list of the clothes he wanted to photograph and the mannequin he thought was the most photogenic. It was my responsibility to organise the photographic sessions and look after each mannequin. I often had to stop any bright young photographer from encouraging the mannequins to rush outside scantily clad in summer or in cocktail wear on a winter's day so that they could take their perfect photograph. There were also security issues to consider. Any mannequin being photographed outside had to be accompanied by a detective as they were often wearing valuable jewellery and furs, making them easy targets for thieves.

Magazines usually had a later release date than newspapers

and the larger magazines made appointments to return to the showroom or borrowed clothes for their own photo shoots. They often took the clothes to be photographed in different settings, such as a country house, a racecourse, a zoo or a museum. There was always great excitement in the workroom when these photographs appeared in the magazines. We all gathered round a copy to see the clothes that we worked so hard on being modelled in different locations.

Straight after the press show, another one was held for buyers from overseas. These buyers were representatives from the large stores in Canada, Australia, South America and the United States who were on the lookout for something new that would capture the market during the next season. They flew to Europe to view the shows and pick the clothes that were best suited to the tastes of clients in their own country. Soon, our clothes appeared in the windows of the most fashionable stores across the world.

Fashion is an international business and I always found it amazing to think that a piece of clothing that I worked on at Lachasse that was bought by an American buyer might have been made from French fabric, trimmed with lace from Switzerland, designed and made in London and shown by a Swedish mannequin in the collection. It could then end up in a store window in New York and might eventually be bought by a British tourist to be worn in London.

Then it was the collection show for the clients, who had been personally invited by a hand written invitation. This was the most important of the shows as it would bring the majority of our day-to-day trade. During the final hour before the show, the *vendeurs* were at the door greeting clients. This required great tact as each client had to be made to feel that they were the most important person at the show. When everyone had arrived, the *vendeurs* began to flutter and chatter nervously as everyone wondered whether the clients would like the new collection. After the show, a stream of questions were asked and the sales staff would be all over the room answering each one. Clothes were rarely purchased at the show. Instead, clients returned later to discuss the collection in detail with the *vendeurs,* make their choices and place their orders.

The experience of my first collection shows gave me an intensive training in the practical side of the fashion trade. My job required careful consideration of all the tiny details and strict delivery dates as well as the ability to think on my feet. I had to make sure that every order was delivered on time. I also had to steer the buyers from one store from ordering exactly the same ensemble as a buyer from a rival store, while at the same time making sure that I did not lose the precious order. The development of a collection was exhausting work and once it was finished we started work on the next collection.

Chapter Nine

The Mannequins

Before there were models, there were mannequins. This was what models were known as when I started in the fashion business. They were elegant and professional and were as perfect as the clothes they wore. When I began my career, a mannequin's work was mainly concentrated into a few weeks in the year during the showing of a collection. Later, with rapid advances in advertising and television, they began to get a steady stream of work all year round and the job of the model became well known. Some of the Lachasse mannequins also modelled in early television shows. After working at Lachasse, they were taken to the BBC production and distribution centre at Alexandra Palace for trials and rehearsals, which very often ran well into the night.

Mannequins entered the fashion world in various ways. Some were daughters of wealthy families whose mothers or relatives introduced them to the fashion houses where they bought their clothes. Others went to one of the well-known modelling schools and took a course in deportment and later found freelance work with a model agency. Out of every hundred would-be mannequins, only a handful ever reached the top of their profession. Their success was not just due to their looks but also to their hard work. It was never an easy job. Once they had committed themselves to their career, the girls needed to show complete professionalism and dedication. They had to be prepared to model fur coats in a heat wave and beachwear in mid-winter. If they took up photographic work, they often had to face the camera and smile outdoors in a silk dress with the temperature near freezing point.

Some of the mannequins from wealthy families didn't need to earn money to support themselves. Often, I found that it was the girl who had the least need to work who was the hardest working. I saw them arrive at Lachasse at 8am ready for a show at 9am. They did two shows before midday, were photographed until 2pm and returned for a show at 3pm and were photographed again until 5pm or 6pm. Then they rushed off home where some of them, like Lois De Vere, then had to bath their children, read bedtime stories and cook dinner.

This has never been a job simply for pretty girls wearing gorgeous clothes. I always saw the mannequins as artists giving a creative touch to the garments they wore. They needed to use their own personality and style in their work. A mannequin could make or break the ensemble she was wearing and it was her own particular way of showing it that charmed all those who come into contact with her. It was she who needed to sell the clothes to clients and the buyers for fashion stores.

A mannequin's reign was a fairly short one but she could be very successful. The work could be difficult and tiring but it could also be rewarding. It was always satisfying to see a mannequin who began at Lachasse as a permanent house mannequin for a few seasons move on to freelance for other fashion houses and then appear on the cover of every glossy magazine. I worked with many famous mannequins, including Bronwen Pugh (later Lady Astor) who was a supermodel of her day, Avril Humphries, who was Mr Michael's muse and always launched the line of the season, and Virginia Woodford. Each of these mannequins was exceptional and modelled with grace and charm.

Some girls married into the best families in England and became distinguished hostesses in society. In 1961, we had a young girl working for us as a house mannequin. She had been in Paris working for Givenchy and had won great acclaim, so when she arrived at Lachasse everyone was delighted. Her petite figure and exotic way of showing pleased Mr Owen, the designer at the time, and soon Carolyn Soley won all the hearts at Lachasse. However, all too soon as far as we were concerned, she was to find the man of her dreams. She married playwright Anthony

Shaffer, twin brother of Peter Shaffer, on 17th December. Their wedding reception was held in the penthouse of the newly opened Carlton Tower Hotel in Belgravia, which had caused quite a stir in the architectural world of post-war London.

Not all mannequins were equally as suitable for the career or displayed the necessary professionalism. Mannequins needed to be on their best behaviour at all times but sometimes they were not entirely committed to their profession. At one lunch party held before an afternoon fashion show at a private house, the host and hostess were generous with their wine. During the afternoon show, I noticed that one mannequin, called Liz, was making some rather exaggerated turns on the catwalk but just thought that she was showing off in front of the audience. We were invited to a sherry party before the evening show and I kept my eye on this particular girl. I soon realised that she was drinking far too much for someone about to appear in an elegant fashion show.

After the party, we were all taken by car to the country house where the evening show was to be held. When we arrived, the host told us about the house's long history and gave us a tour. Liz was by now too drunk to make the tour, so we left her behind. When the tour was over, we began to prepare for the evening show but there was no sign of Liz anywhere. I retraced our route around the house and found Liz fast asleep on a four-poster bed in one of the grandest bedrooms. Just then our hostess entered with another guest and I hastily drew the curtains round the sleeping girl. Our hostess, keen to illustrate a point she was making about the history of the house, pulled the curtains back with a flourish revealed Liz.

'I suppose,' remarked one of the guests, 'this is Elizabeth I see sleeping there – or is it the sleeping beauty?'

I explained what had happened as tactfully as I could and we left her to sleep it off. There was no possibility of her being fit for the show that evening. I told everyone that Liz was unwell and we changed the order of the show. I don't think anyone ever knew the true story but I made sure Liz was never booked again.

Once a fashion show was over, mannequins often revealed

their sense of fun and mischief. At one charity show held in the North of England, the hostess announced that a large after-show party would take place at a nearby house. Everything had been arranged. We would be driven there by the committee members and that officers from a local barracks had been invited to escort the mannequins. When all the work was finished and the clothes packed away, the mannequins re-did their makeup and, as is always the custom at Lachasse, put on their favourite dress from the collection to wear to the party.

The evening seemed to go well. The supper was gastronomic and the champagne flowed. The officers arrived dressed in their spotless and starched uniforms and were introduced to the mannequins. It was obvious to all onlookers that they thought they were in for a good time. Everyone seemed to get on well and, at the end of the party, pens and paper were produced and addresses and telephone numbers exchanged.

Travelling back to London by coach the next day, there was more laughter and chatter than usual. I asked some of the girls whether they enjoyed the party and what they thought of their male escorts.

'Are you looking forward to getting a phone call?' I asked one girl.

'That would be a long wait!' She laughed.

Apparently, they had given the numbers of all kinds of shops and businesses to the men. I wonder what kind of response the officers got when they rang those numbers looking for their dream girl.

Chapter Ten

Fashion Shows

Lachasse's fashion shows weren't just limited to those held at our premises and we toured our collections to hotels, stately homes and other venues across the country and around the world. We showed wedding dresses, formal wear, outdoor and sporting wear to crowds of eager potential clients. We visited beautiful locations and I mingled with celebrities and dignities of the era. They were often glamorous events but they were also hard work and great care went into the preparations, as there was always potential for things to go wrong.

One of the stars of many of the shows was Miss Lachasse, one of our most treasured possessions. She was a doll made in July 1954 by Mr Owens and the staff at Lachasse in response to a request from wartime heroine Odette Churchill. The doll was made exactly to scale from the measurements of Virginia Woodford, a resident mannequin for several seasons. She had a complete wardrobe of clothes, everything that a couture client would buy, including a fur coat, lingerie, accessories and shoes. Each item had been designed by a leading name in the fashion trade and all were made with the same skill that would be put into a garment or accessory purchased by a client. The doll was one of the exhibits at the 'Unique Dolls Through the Ages' exhibition, held at 45 Park Lane in the '50s. She created a sensation at the exhibition and drew great interest from the media and the large crowds who flocked to the show. When Lachasse closed, Virginia was given to the Bath Museum of Costume and Textile and she was later exhibited at 'The Golden Age of Couture' exhibition at the Victoria and Albert Museum.

After much preliminary planning, the designer and Director at Lachasse were usually invited to the house or hall at which the show would take place. They needed to look at the rooms that were going to be used for the showings, choose the dressing rooms and see that the necessary food and accommodation could be provided. Everyone needed plenty of rest and refreshments after the show. We worked hard and most of the time we were running on little more than nervous energy.

Once we were satisfied with the arrangements, the mannequins were chosen and booked. One by one, they called at Lachasse to try the clothes and hats. As with the shows held in the house, furs, gloves, jewellery and tights were ordered and each girl was given an appointment at the hairdressers. Then, an order of showing was prepared. This was one of the most difficult tasks, for each girl needed to have enough time to show the clothes, return to the improvised dressing room, change and be ready to show again. Somehow, after a great deal of thought, the list was finished and was sent to the organising committee at the venue so they could approve the programme and have it professionally printed and also circulate the times to their own helpers.

Next, the assistant designer was given the list of mannequins detailing what each was to wear, so that each garment could be given its own label together with the mannequin's name. When this job was complete, the label was fixed to the appropriate coat hanger and, on the morning of the show, large clothes racks were placed in the showroom. The head showroom junior was given the task of hanging the correct gown or coat on its respective hanger. They had to see that each garment was in perfect condition and neatly pressed. All shoes, tights and gloves had to be spotless. Every trimming had to be securely fastened and every button sewn on correctly. The millinery department packed the hats into large trunks. When everything was ready, there was a roll call by the Director, while the collection was loaded into the vans. The coach arrived, and the mannequins, dressers and the rest of the entourage got ready for the journey.

The chatter and excitement on the coach was more like a

holiday than a day's work. Many of the houses we visited were near London but others were as far away as Cumberland, Wales and Norfolk and then we had to stay overnight. When this happened, each person was found a bed in a home carefully selected by the committee. When we arrived at our destination, the host and hostess met us and, after all the goods had been unpacked, the staff were taken to their temporary homes for a meal and a good night's rest.

The next day, everyone met for a run-through so that timings could be finalised and any necessary changes made. The mannequins had to familiarise themselves with their surroundings and navigate their way through houses that often weren't really suitable for a fashion show. They often had to contend with several flights of stairs, highly polished floors and dimly lit corridors. All these could be a nightmare for a mannequin wearing high-heeled shoes and possibly a voluminous gown. The atmosphere backstage could become quite stormy as mannequins protested that it was impossible to climb two flights of narrow stairs, undressing as they went, and be ready to re-enter in just three minutes. Things usually worked themselves out, details were rearranged and the run through would usually end with everyone excited about the upcoming show.

The mannequins then departed to their dressing rooms, together with the helpers and hairdressers. The jewellers took up their positions, the furrier sorted out his furs and a detective arrived to guard the valuables. Most of the backstage organisation was left to me. I had to make sure that the gloves were laid out, the hats assembled, the jeweller had a table and a mirror and there was enough space for each person to work at top speed once the show started. It was also my responsibility to keep any local boys away from the girls as they were changing. Once the show was over, we could relax again and join in the lavish parties that were often held afterwards.

At these shows, I was introduced to some of the most elegant people of the day while experiencing some of the most wonderful surroundings in the country. In October 1960, we held a show at Blickling Hall in Norfolk in aid of the British Red Cross and the

Distressed Gentlefolk's Aid Association. It was opened by the Viscountess Lewisham, later Countess Spencer and stepmother of Diana, Princess of Wales. Blickling Hall, a large red-brick Jacobean mansion built in 1620 by the Earl of Buckingham's family, was one of the most beautiful houses of its period. In 1940, the 11th Marquess of Lothian left the hall and 4,500 acres to the National Trust. The 1627 Jacobean ceiling inspired Mr Owen, the designer at Lachasse, to create a pale green silk ball gown embroidered in topaz stones, which followed the ceiling's design. A supper party was held after the evening show in a marquee in the grounds and we were surrounded by peacocks strutting and fanning their tails. It was a glamorous end to all our hard work.

We held many shows at Cliveden, the country home of Lord and Lady Astor. This had been a fashionable place for politicians and artists to meet in the '30s and had been the setting of many lavish parties. Lady Astor was a perfect hostess and, during a break in one fashion show, she provided bathing costumes for everyone so that we could make use of her own private indoor swimming pool. This was greatly appreciated by the mannequins who were wilting in the mid-summer heat. It was a gesture prompted by Lady Astor's own experience of working as a mannequin in London and in Paris for the house of Balmain before her marriage.

Fashion shows could be glamorous and enchanting social occasions but for the Lachasse staff they were always hard work as we were responsible for everything running smoothly. Sometimes everything did not go exactly according to plan and sometimes little mistakes could lead to big problems. This was the case during a press show we held at Garrards, the court jewellers. The collection was shown together with furs provided by Calman Links and a million pounds worth of jewels. The press were only allowed in by numbered invitations, which were closely checked at the door. A large queue formed outside the jewellers and stretched down Regent Street and had to be kept in order by the police. The mannequins dressed on the first floor and descended by way of a sweeping staircase to the ground floor, where the press were seated surrounded by glass show-cases full of priceless jewels. The showing was followed by a champagne supper and each mannequin was allowed to mingle with the press while wearing an evening gown and jewels. One mannequin, when pulling off her glove, forgot that she was wearing a valuable ring on top and the ring flew off unnoticed. It was not missed until after the show when the jewellery was checked. It was a disaster and everyone was a suspect. No one was allowed to leave until the ring had been found. The doors were sealed by the security guards and the search began. It wasn't until later when the ring was found under one of the showcases, where it had fallen, that the party could resume.

At another fashion show held in Garrards, the main staircase was again used as part of the catwalk. As she was descending, one mannequin missed her footing and, as she fell, muttered a stream of four letter words, while a microphone relayed her feelings to the crowd.

Not all venues were to our liking and some were completely unsuitable for a fashion show. We were booked by people eager to have a fashion show at their event but who didn't consider what exactly that entailed. On one occasion, I arrived with a mannequin to give a small fashion show for a guild. When we arrived, after a long journey, we found that the guild met in an upstairs room of a local inn where there had been a disco the night before. The room was a mess and chairs were strewn everywhere. There was a small stage at one end of the hall but this was piled high with tables and two tired looking curtains hung from a rail. Sheena, the mannequin, was always a profes-sional and took a broom and swept the stage, rearranged the tables to make a place to sit, and asked for a mirror. The guild secretary had totally forgotten about our small list of necessi-tates and so ran home to see what she could gather.

I began to arrange the chairs in rows and various guild members started to arrive but they were more interested in arranging a display of trophies around the stage than helping. Eventually, the secretary returned with a large cheval glass. Sheena dressed and put the finishing touches to her make-up.

In no time, the room filled up and extra chairs were brought in. Madam Chairman made an opening speech and the show began.

What we did not realise straight away was that the hall was directly over the inn kitchens. Although all was peaceful at the start of the evening, as soon as people began to order food the kitchens sprang into life. I can only imagine that everyone had ordered a fry-up that night. Smoke filtered up through the floorboards and soon filled the air. We could not open the doors or windows because of the noise of customers arriving at the restaurant. The show must go on and so on we went. I coughed and spluttered, Sheena wiped her eyes carefully, trying not to smudge her make-up. The audience, however, seemed to take all this in their stride and listened intently to my every spluttered word.

When the show ended, I was terrified that all the clothes would smell of fried fat the next day but when I checked them there was no smell at all.

I asked Sheena, who burst out laughing and said. 'Just as soon as I took them off, I put them straight back into their cellophane bags and sealed them up away from the smoke.'

Her quick thinking saved some expensive gowns.

'But,' she continued, 'I was the one who got cured that night. I have bathed a dozen times since I got home but I still smell like a piece of bacon.'

Chapter Eleven

Charity Work

The fashion industry may seem like a glamorous one, full of exquisite dresses and beautiful people but many of us within it work hard to raise money for charity. During my early career, the wartime ethic of raising money for those less fortunate than yourself was still strong and many people contributed in some way to charity. Everyone at Lachasse was involved in organising fashion shows to raise money for a whole range of charities, from the Red Cross to those supporting individual projects. The majority of the showroom staff gave up their own time to help with the preparations and worked tirelessly to make these events a success. From early in my career, I dedicated myself to charity work. I had been given so many opportunities in life that I wanted to give something back. It became a way of life to devote time to good causes.

In December 1959, Lachasse was asked to give a gala fashion show in aid of the Family Service Unit, an organisation that helped underprivileged families. It was held on a cold, wet winter's evening at the home of Mrs Susan Blythe in Hamilton Terrace, St John's Wood. Mrs Blythe opened up the whole of the house and allowed the mannequins to dress upstairs and to model the clothes in all the rooms downstairs. The organising committee had worked hard and the evening was completely sold out. It was a glamorous event with many exquisitely dressed women in attendance. Virginia Lyon wore a mink peruke and a tiara and Penelope Alsopp wore a chinchilla jacket. The other guests included the singer Alma Cogan who arrived wearing a full-length mink coat and swept into her seat in the front row.

Dudley Moore played the piano and pianist Winifred Atwell beamed with approval. The evening ended with a buffet supper and congratulations were handed round like bouquets on a gala night. Swept up in all the excitement, plans were made immediately to follow the show with another.

Sally Simpson and Virginia Lyon immediately took charge of planning the next event. St Swithins School in Winchester was about to celebrate its 75th anniversary with an appeal in March 1960 and asked Lachasse to organise a show. So, we boarded the coach once again, taking jewels, furs and the collection, together with mannequins and some staff. Sally and Virginia had very definite ideas about how the show should be structured and it was split into sportswear, including bikinis, which in the '60s were still considered *avant garde*, gowns and furs. Sally Simpson arranged to bring Boscoe Holder's steel band from the Mayfair Hotel and they gave their services for free. It was a huge success and a great deal of money was raised for the school funds.

We travelled all over Britain to support charities and, in October 1966, I found myself taking the night train to Haddo House in Aberdeen to help to raise money for their Choral Society. On arrival at Aberdeen Station, we were met by Lord Haddo, the Marquis of Aberdeen, and Captain Wolrige-Gordon and were split into smaller parties to be driven through the Scottish countryside to Haddo House. Haddo House had been built in 1731 by William Adam, the father of the Adam brothers to replace the old house of Kellie, which had housed the Gordons of Methick for centuries. I was looking forward to seeing it for myself. The show was in aid of Haddo House Choral Society, which Lady Haddo had started in 1944, and was a great success with an audience of over 500 people. Lady Haddo showed us over the house and let us in on many of its secret features, including a staircase hidden behind a bookcase in the library leading down to the private chapel. The Lachasse staff were made to feel part of the family and we ate all our meals with the Haddos and Lord Haddo took us on walks round the estate. When it was time to leave, nearly all the family and staff gathered in front of the house to wave us goodbye with white handkerchiefs – a custom which we were told meant that you wished your guests to return. It was a charming gesture after a memorable weekend.

I worked alongside many fascinating people to raise money for good causes. In the 1960s, Margot, Countess of Buckinghamshire, was one of the leading hostesses in London and a great force behind many charity events. It was a great honour and pleasure to work alongside her. Charity work also proved to be a good opportunity to make new friends. When Emma Kitchener, grand-daughter of Lord Kitchener, was in her teens we met while working annually at the Spring Ball, raising money for Westminster Mencap and the Royal Marsden Hospital playroom appeal. Tall, elegant Emma would arrive full of ideas and suggestions. She later married Julian Fellowes, who would go on to win an Oscar for his script of 'Gosford Park', and we all became friends.

I was involved with organising many charity performances and could always rely on my friends to help. In 1972, when organising a performance for Marcel Marceau, the French mime, to raise money for the Deaf Institute, I asked a great friend living in Basil Street to be the chairman of the event. She agreed and asked what she should do to prepare. I said that it was usual for the chairperson to give a launching party. She agreed to this and decided to hold the party in her own flat. When I arrived to help prepare for the party, she asked me to go into the bathroom, where she had stored the champagne, to see whether she had bought enough. When I entered the bathroom, I was faced with a bath full to overflowing with bottles of champagne. Needless to say the party went well that night.

Many London venues were incredibly generous in offering us space to hold charity events. In the 1960s, one of my favourite ones was the Martini Terrazza at New Zealand House on Haymarket, which offered magnificent views over London landmarks such as Trafalgar Square, the Houses of Parliament, Buckingham Palace and the bridges over the river Thames. The manager, Mrs Howard, often let me use the glamorous Terrazza, with full hospitality, for my charity events. When the Terrazza closed, it was a great loss to London's fundraising effort.

The Goldsmith's Hall of the City of London made another wonderful venue for any event, as we found when we held a fashion show there in 1978 in aid of the Friends of Cheyne Centre for Spastic Children and the Handicapped Adventure Play-ground Association. Flanked by the gold plate belonging to the Worshipful Company of Goldsmiths, the mannequins paraded down the length of the room. No artificial spot lighting was needed as the light falling from exquisite chandeliers hanging from the ceiling set the mood perfectly. The Duchess of Gloucester graced the occasion and took great interest both in the clothes we were showing and the two charities we were supporting. It was a grand and glamorous occasion from the moment the royal party was greeted by two state trumpeters until the end when we learned how much money we had raised.

Another of London's historic buildings, the Banqueting House in Whitehall, was the venue for a fashion show, which Lachasse was asked to give in aid of The Soldier's, Sailors' and Airmen's Families Association. Lt General Sir Reginald Denning was the organiser, assisted by Bella Newman, the Director of Appeals, and the committee was chaired by the Duchess of St Albans. I worked many times with Suzanne St Albans before she left England to live and write in her flat overlooking the harbour at Monte Carlo and to continue her great love of travel. Generous with her hospitality, she also gave freely her time and efforts to many charities and her departure left a huge void. On this occasion, the committee worked hard and all the seats were sold out in no time. The guest of honour was Princess Margaret, who looked stunning in a dress of gold tissue. The evening was a huge success and raised a very large sum for the SSAFA.

I was even lucky enough to hold charity events in some well known political venues. Through Ken and Gillian Clarke, who were always eager to help deserving charities, I was able to hold fund raising cocktail parties at No 11 Downing Street. Through Betty Boothroyd, I was given permission to hold the first fashion show ever held in Speakers House in aid of the Marie Curie Fund.

Lachasse also raised money for charities through donating clothes to fashion jumble sales. These were a chance for people to pick up a bargain and we could sell our unwanted or left over clothes. Sometimes customers became a little over excited at the prospect of finding a Lachasse garment in one of these jumble sales. A German countess, who helped on one of the charity jumble sale committees, found a rather tired chiffon evening gown which I had donated among the sale rails and bought it straight away. At the next gala evening I attended, I saw her wafting up and down the room wearing the evening dress. In fact, I was to see it many more times over the next six or seven years. Whenever she supported my efforts for charity, she always wore the dress and insisted on telling everyone around that it was her one and only Lachasse dress and that it had been designed especially for her by me. At another jumble sale, a client bought several dresses and arrived at my flat later that evening for supper wearing one of the bargain dresses straight off the jumble rail without having sent it to the cleaners.

One evening in the early '60s, I was invited to a small supper party on Paultons Square, Chelsea. The hostess told me about her friend who worked for a makeup company who she felt that I should meet as we had a good deal in common. The meeting was arranged and I was apprehensive and wondered exactly what we had in common as she had given me no further information. As soon as I arrived, my hostess took me over to a group where a blonde woman sat talking animatedly to the other guests. When I had the opportunity to speak to her alone, I found that our lives and careers had many similarities.

Eve Gardiner worked for Max Factor and ran their Bond Street salon, having been with the company since 1938. She knew almost everyone on the London stage, in the theatre world and those in the film industry. She had travelled widely and had often been to Hollywood to meet the stars and to study the methods used in the makeup studios. She was devoted to her job and it was an integral part of her life. As well as being a talented and enthusiastic makeup artist, she was committed to helping others and put her talents and experience to good use. She worked on providing and applying makeup for many badly burned victims of the Second World War and gave lectures on makeup to the blind. We spent the whole evening deep in conversation and it sowed the seeds of a mutual interest in using the skills developed in our careers to help others and of a lasting friendship.

It was though Eve that I first became interested in doing charity work for the blind. I volunteered to make dozens of broadcasts and tapes, which were aimed at helping blind people to live independent lives. These explained to people how to use makeup and how to shop for clothes by themselves with the knowledge of what was fashionable at the time. I began to realise that I could use my specific skills and background to help other people to enjoy fashion. Later, I helped to organise giant jumble sales to raise money to fund similar projects and for many years I found myself running two of these events a year – one in the spring for the blind and one in autumn for Cancer Research.

These jumble shows were often frantic occasions. Upon hearing that I worked in fashion, women would pester me to give them advice about what to buy or which outfit best suited them. On one occasion, we used the Old Town Hall in the Kings Road, Chelsea, and many friends in the literary and stage world supported us. Beryl Cook, Dilys Powell, Anna Dawson, Doris Leslie, Barbara Cartland and Ursula Bloom were just a few of our kind supporters who spent hours signing photographs and books.

As I assumed more responsibilities at Lachasse, Eve offered to organise the makeup for our shows. Each season we would work together and create a new look, combining both clothes and makeup. When the Bond Street salon closed in 1974 and Eve semi-retired, she asked me to pop in and see her before the final day. Sitting at her desk, she looked just as glamorous as a young woman of thirty. She handed me a small, elegantly wrapped package, which I opened it on the spot. Inside, I found a small gilt casket. I lifted the lid and smelled the amber wax inside. It had a curious smell. Eve watched my expression.

'What does it remind you of?' she asked.

I sniffed it again. 'Why,' I said, 'a church.'

'How clever!' she remarked. 'It was inspired by the smell of the candles and incense of Notre-Dame in Paris. It took years to produce, but, now we have managed it, the perfume will last forever.'

All these years later, I still have the box and, whenever I lift the lid, memories of my trips to Paris in the '50s and '60s come flooding back. The name of the scent was 'Lachasse'.

Alongside working at Lachasse, I continued to spend my time raising money for charity. I was lucky enough to be able to use my passion and talents to benefit people outside the fashion world. One of the charities that I always supported was the Mission to Deep Sea Fishermen. I organised many charity events on their behalf, including one at the Mermaid Inn in Rye, where Betty Boothroyd was guest of honour. This ancient inn was once used by smugglers and was full of antique furniture, including four poster beds, secret passages and a resident ghost. It was a magical location and Lady Shawcross generously opened her house and Japanese garden for the guests.

I received many honours and awards for my charity work. In 1976, I was nominated by the Vice President of the National Institute of Social Sciences in New York to be an Honorary Member. This was an association set up in 1865 by a group of Boston's leading citizens to bring together people to try and solve the country's social problems. It was comprised of one thousand members across America and a few in the rest of the world. I was honoured to be included. By the time of my presentation, only four other Englishmen had been given the honour – Walter Lessing, Sir Francis Evans, Sir Edwin Leather and Bill Ormerod. Many other distinguished people had been the recipients of the Gold Medal, including Madame Marie Curie, Claire Booth Luce, Dean Rush, Bob Hope, Danny Kaye, and Henry Kissinger. When I asked Mrs Archdeacon, the President, why she had proposed me for the honour, she told me that it was for the work that I did outside my profession. I always felt that my work outside Lachasse was of wider value and it felt wonderful that this had been recognised.

I was honoured to be granted Freedom of the City of London

in 1978, at one of the oldest surviving traditional ceremonies still in existence today. I am also a Trustee of the Museum of Gardening. I later became a member of the Guild of Freemen of the City of London and was invited to join the Court of the Guild of Freemen of the City of London and am now Senior Warden of the Guild. In 1998, I was awarded the OBE for my charity work and my professional work, followed by the Stanley Pritchard Award in 2007 for my support of The Royal National Mission to Deep Sea Fishermen and my work as Vice Patron. I treasure all these awards and honours and am proud that I was able to build so successfully on the charity work that I started during my boyhood in Hunstanton.

Chapter Twelve

My Clients

Every man has a type of woman he admires above all others. She may be plump, slim, dark or fair but she is his type.

Quite often people ask me, 'Who was the client you liked dressing the most?'

To this, I always reply, 'The one who pays her bills.'

This is of course not quite true. It is hard for me to describe exactly the type of woman I liked to dress. She needed to be interested in clothes and listen to the advice I gave her, even if she did not take it. I preferred dressing women who were above the age of twenty-six rather than those younger, simply because they were more definite in their views. By the age of twenty-six, most women have tried many styles and understand what suits their figure.

I always took great pride in knowing that my clients could be wearing the clothes I made for them ten years later. Although the clothes may no longer be fashionable, the client would still look well dressed. I was always infuriated by untidy dressing. Women should always spend a few moments each day to see that their clothes are well brushed, pressed and free from grease spots. I know it is difficult to look immaculate at all times but it takes very little time to look tidy and presentable.

While fashion is a business, it should also be fun. Once you realise that, both client and salesperson enjoy fittings and the clothes much more. My policy in the showroom was that when a client came to Lachasse she should be made to feel that the visit was something special. Whenever she wore the garment in the future she would have the confidence of all the happy memories.

A friend of mine who was a *vendeuse* in another London fashion house always treated the whole business with such a grim attitude. I was sure the clients she served bought their clothes from her out of simple necessity rather than pleasure. I saw things very differently. I always tried to put the client at ease so that she felt welcome as soon as she entered the showroom. At the first meeting, I usually chatted about whoever had recommended her to me so that she knew that she was among friends. The clients in a fashion house like Lachasse became more like friends and tended to use the house as a club. This was encouraged for no one expected a client to buy every time she passed through the doors. As I grew to know a client, and her family and circle of friends, it was always very satisfying to have her pop in for a chat and a cup of coffee when up in town.

One season, a client might need many new clothes. Perhaps she, or her husband, had taken up an office or was about to embark on some public work and so needed several complete ensembles. Or perhaps, she had been invited to a wedding or was going on a cruise, for which she would need some new outfits. In these circumstances, I would see a client many times over a short period of time. I would sit with them, discuss their forthcoming engagements and select suitable ensembles. I had to be prepared for anything. A client might be going on a business trip with her husband and needed clothes to wear in New York in the fall. Then, she might be going on a round the world cruise and so would need clothes suitable for Cairo, Istanbul or Moscow. I was expected to know what type of clothes, texture, weight and colour she would need in each country and so I developed great knowledge of geography. I acquired a huge range of information from all the individual requirement of each client who came through the doors.

When holidaying in the South of France, in August 1958, I received an urgent phone call one lunchtime from Lachasse. A client living close to Farm Street had been in to place a large order but was waiting for me to return before making her final choices. The matter was urgent, as her husband was to be appointed to a new post and she wanted the clothes to be ready as soon as possible. I decided to cut my holiday short and fly back to sort things out. I was intrigued as to what this important post was. Two days later, the client came to see me and we finalised her choices. The next day, all was made clear in the national press. Her husband was to be Lord Chief Justice, and she, Kentucky-born Lady Parker, would in the future have a very full schedule of events to attend.

One day, Lady Parker came to see me to say that she was organising a ball at the Mansion House with dancing in the newly restored Egyptian Room. Princess Margaret was to be Guest of Honour. As the theme was to be Georgian, Lady Parker wanted me to design a fancy dress costume for her based on the period between 1714 and 1820. It had to be correct for the period, suitable for her style and something that she could wear again in the future. I needed to do some research and visited the Victoria and Albert Museum to make some sketches from their displays. From these sketches, Lady Parker chose an apricot stain dress in the Empire style, trimmed with bold beads and pearls. There was great excitement in the workrooms as several clients came in to order dresses for themselves and their daughters for the ball. The whole evening turned out to be a dazzling affair. Princess Margaret arrived in a dress designed by Oliver Messel and Lord Snowden wore a beautiful Georgian costume, also designed by Oliver Messel. The cabaret was provided by Cilla Black, then at the peak of her singing career. The evening made a huge amount of money towards the rebuilding of the blitzed church of St John's in Smith Square, Westminster

In my career, I was lucky enough to dress many important and dignified women. In January 1969, Dr Marjorie Blackie, then in her sixties, was the first woman to be appointed physician to the Queen and several other members of the royal family. She came from a family of homoeopathic doctors and her uncle, Dr Compton Burnett, was the father of Dame Ivy, the author. Dr Blackie and her two sisters, Mrs Townsend and Miss Blackie, came to Lachasse and, with her natural charms, Dr Blackie was loved by the staff.

Her life-long friend, Miss Musette Majendie, kept a style of her own and always made sure that her tailored clothes had plenty of walking space. Miss Majendie was essentially a countrywoman who enjoyed many outdoor activities. Her great interest was working with the local Boy Scouts at Hedingham, near to her home at Hedingham castle, and she became the first ever female scout leader. I tried on more than one occasion to make her promise not to take the scout troop out trekking in one of the suits I had just made for her. Great attention was given to her hats, which, when finished, were often thrown into the back of the car to be mistakenly sat on later.

I designed evening gowns for both Dr Blackie and Miss Majendie and, when wearing them, they were the epitome of the English woman after dark. Their naturally graceful movements gave the dresses an elegance all designers long to see. They were stylish women but sometimes had some unusual approaches to fashion. On one occasion, Miss Majendie brought in a Queen Anne bed cover to Lachasse and insisted that I cut it up and design an evening dress suitable for this magnificent fabric. The fabric was so delicate that it had to be carefully mounted on to a backing to stop it splitting when it was sewn. I worked long and hard on that dress and when it was finished it was worn at a reception at the Guildhall where the Queen was present.

Dr Blackie and Miss Majendie were very generous in their hospitality and often invited me to social events. I visited Hedingham Castle for a ball in 1965, bringing Miss Joyce, Mr Todd and a girlfriend of mine to make up a party of four. When we asked Dr Blackie for some kind of landmark, which we could look for as we approached the castle, we were told that a red light would be placed in one of the turrets to help guests find their way in the dark countryside. Off we set from London in a happy, expectant mood. On and on we drove into the Essex countryside, keeping a watchful eye for the red beacon. Our spirits were high as we drew nearer to our landmark and finally arrived to find ourselves not at Hedingham Castle but at a local airport where Miss Joyce, who was driving, obtained much more accurate details of our route to Hedingham. Once there, all difficulties were forgotten and we spent another happy and elegant evening in wonderful surroundings.

I have enjoyed dressing a great many women but I did have a few special favourites. One of these women, due to her elegance and charm was Catherine Walston, the wife of the life peer Lord Walston. She had a natural elegance and a casual smartness that was the envy of every mannequin at Lachasse. There were a few women who always seemed untouched by the demands of a busy life and knew exactly what would suit them. One was Nellie, the Baroness Burton, who possessed a sincere frankness and a love of clothes. Others were Lady Dovercourt, who always looked faultless, and Lady Joan Cator, who always demanded that her clothes never looked *outré* but always conformed. Lady Fisher, formerly Maria Elsner, a star in Ivor Novello's 'The Dancing Years', had quite the most beautiful blue eyes I have ever seen. They were like large star sapphires and she was always a joy to dress. We often made suits for the elegant Princess Marina, the late Duchess of Kent, and for the ex-Queen Mother of Rumania. Both quickly put the staff at ease by their charm and their knowledge of exactly what suited them.

Another lady of great and simple elegance was Mrs Strickland Hubbard. Her superb taste and natural poise made her a designer's delight and her great patience was a joy to the fitters. It was always my pleasure to serve the late Countess Mountbatten of Burma as she always knew exactly what she wanted. While fitting, she would discuss whether the ensemble she was trying on would be suitable for her forthcoming engagements.

I remember her on one occasion turning to me and asking, 'Well, Mr Crown, what shall I do?'

I urged her to buy the suit she was trying on, at which she laughed and said, 'That is exactly what I wanted to hear you say. Now I can always blame you for my extravagance!'

Margaret Campbell, Duchess of Argyle, a well known society figure, was always impeccably dressed and, for one of her trips abroad, Lachasse made her a completely white wardrobe. It was stunning and very different from her usual black town wear. She had a style all of her own and was wise enough to keep to it as she knew how well it suited her. Whenever she came to Lachasse, she brought her pet poodle who she loved dearly.

Another client whom it was always a pleasure to dress was Lady Butler, of Saffron Walden, formerly Mrs Courtauld. I had always made clothes for her daughter, Mrs Fordham, so it was no surprise when they both came to see the collection one afternoon. She told me that she was looking for something to wear at a wedding and asked me for my suggestions. It became clear that this was to be a quiet wedding in a country with no fuss.

As we talked and the mannequins paraded, she suddenly turned to me and said, 'I know, Mr Crown, that I can trust you. It's for my own wedding but I want to keep it quiet and in fact some of my family haven't been told about it yet.'

I was thrilled to be entrusted with this secret and kept it so well that not even the fitters knew about the wedding. All the clothes were finished long before the press had any idea that the Home Secretary was about to be married again. Once the news was out, I was hounded by reporters, especially after the bride gave an interview and said that she was dressed exclusively by Lachasse. Later, at the time of the wedding of Princess Margaret, the press besieged me again, looking for details of what several of my clients would be wearing and how much they had spent – a matter which is always a secret between client and *vendeuse* and no one else.

Clothes can make their wearer feel many different emotions and almost every woman feels special with a new dress. I saw this illustrated when clients bought garments for special occasions or were given them as gifts. In the Lachasse showroom, I was often able to see the relationships between my clients and their loved ones and how this was displayed by the clothes they bought. Once, Sir George Schuster, who was the oldest member of Lincoln's Inn and one of only four former MPs to reach a century when he died in June 1982, paid a sudden visit to see me at Lachasse. He asked what kind of a garment I thought his wife would like as a birthday present. We talked about events they had coming up at their home in Middle Barton, Oxfordshire, and finally decided that a tweed topcoat and matching skirt would be of the greatest use. He handed me a cheque in settlement of the garments and left. Several weeks later, Lady Schuster arrived for a fitting. Sir George had presented her with a fitting card on her birthday and she had no idea what the actual gift was. Luckily, she approved of our choice and was delighted at such a gift. It was a very happy experience to see two people who were obviously still very much in love spoiling each other in the later years of their lives.

On another occasion, an elderly client came to see us immediately after her husband's funeral service and, while the car and chauffeur waited outside, she looked at the new clothes. I said how sorry I was to hear the sad news and offered my condolences.

'Enough of that,' said the woman. 'I have come to be cheered up!'

She then ordered four brightly coloured dresses and insisted that one should be in red. The only thing I could think of was that perhaps she wanted to give her late husband a good send-off.

It was always interesting when new clients arrived at Lachasse to see what they would order and whether they would become life-long regulars like so many of our clients. One lunchtime, I was called to chat to a prospective client. She was rather small, neat and on the shy side. I chose some garments for the mannequins to show her and after a while she quietly asked me to quote prices. This I did and she left saying that her employer would visit us shortly. I assumed that this was just a way of leaving gracefully, without buying, and forgot about the incident. However, a few weeks later the showroom door was opened by an elegant man, who asked for me by name. He told me that shortly Lady Abbassi would be arriving to see some clothes and asked me to make the necessary arrangements. With that he left and ten minutes later a most attractive woman arrived, followed by several people, including four young ladies. I showed them to the salon, and Lady Abbassi sat at the centre. After the collection had been shown, she handed me a list of the items she wished to order, which amounted to quite a large proportion of the collection. Measurements were taken and during that season when Carol, the step-daughter to His Highness the Ameer of Bahawalpur, came out, I saw a great deal of her ladyship and her family.

My first encounters with clients did not always run quite so smoothly. One day, I was called to the telephone and, not concentrating, thought I had been told that it was one of mannequins called Tina who had called. She was one of the oldest mannequins at the time, but always looking for work, so I used to tease her and call her 'Granny'. Picking up the telephone, I gave her some tirade of nonsense about being too old to work and finished by suggesting it was about time she retired.

Back came the voice at the other end, 'No, Mr Crown. It is not Tina but Dina.'

Again not listening, I carried on with my joking when it suddenly struck me that the voice was quite different from Tina's.

To my horror I heard a plaintive voice struggling to say, 'No, no, Mr Crown. It is not Tina, but Dina of Jordan.'

I gasped and apologised profusely, as the voice went on.

'This is Princess Dina of Jordan. I am telephoning you from Jordan as I am planning to fly to London tomorrow to see you and to order some clothes.'

I repeated my apologies even more effusively and said that it would be my pleasure to welcome her to Lachasse.

When she arrived she smiled at once, realising what had happened, and remarked, 'I am delighted to know that you have a good sense of humour.'

She brought her daughter, Princess Alia al Hussein, who ordered her first outfit from Lachasse. She was the same age that Princess Dina had been when she came to Lachasse to order clothes for her trousseau when she married King Hussein of Jordan.

There were many times in the social calendar when we at Lachasse would be busy and the showroom would be full of women wanting clothes for a special occasion. One of the most important events in the social calendar was Ascot. Once the spring and summer collection was shown in February, clients would be thinking ahead to the royal race meeting, held in the middle of June. As the weeks and months flew past, the tempo quickened gradually until it reached a climax in about the first week of June. Tempers ran high in the workrooms, working hours became longer and there was a great surge of activity to get both the clothes and the hats ready for Ascot week. It was a nerve-racking time for all concerned but somehow every year everything was finished and delivered on time.

I was lucky enough to take the four afternoons of Ascot week off work every year. I would rush down to the racecourse and enjoy a quiet meal with friends. Then, I could relax and see the fashions displayed, as they should be – on elegant women in perfect surroundings. I always cast a critical eye on my own work, judging some outfits as successful and some as perhaps less so. The unsuccessful outfits were often due to the way the client had accessorised her ensemble. Sometimes, she had simply put the hat on at the wrong angle. It always took a great strength of mind to stop myself from sidling over and giving it a tweak. Afterwards, I often had to race back to teach in London wearing my Ascot clothes, much to delight of my students who were always interested to know how the days went. Miss Pemberton, head of the fashion department, encouraged this and believed that it was important for the students to see how garments would be worn.

When society events were held, many of our clients were invited and Lachasse's showroom became extremely busy. If there were to be a party or ball, we often made many of the gowns for the guests. One splendid fancy dress ball in which we were involved was held in June 1965 at the Royal Courts of Justice in the Strand. This was the first time in history that permission had been given for such an event there. The great hall was used as the centrepiece in celebration of the 150th anniversary of the Battle of Waterloo. Lachasse was kept busy for weeks making dresses for all our clients who had been invited. One memorable gown was a shell pink jersey empire dress, softly draped with a small train, for Lady Parker. Madam Nubar Gulbenkian was resplendent in an elegant evening gown, wearing the fabulous

Gulbenkian emeralds, and the guest of honour was Princess Grace of Monaco. The whole event created great interest and the national newspapers carried sketches, details and photographs of the guests wearing their costumes. With the help of the television interviewer John Tidmarsh, I was given the job of describing the guest's arrival on television.

The following year saw one of the most notable society weddings of the '60s. On 6th July, Jane Leverhulme married Algernton Heber-Percy, the Duke of Northumberland's cousin, at the Guard's Chapel, Wellington Barracks. The reception for a thousand guests was the first private function to be held at Lancaster House for forty-six years. I had the enjoyable task of designing the wedding dress, which was made at Lachasse. The veil was to be held in place by a tiara made of magnificent diamonds, one of the family heirlooms. Lady Leverhulme had expressed some concerns about this tiara which, like many old ones, could be split into several pieces to be used as brooches or clips. During the various fittings, we realised that we needed a safe place to put the tiara when she left on her honeymoon. Ever eager to help a client, I offered to take it with me back to Lachasse, where it could be collected later.

At the appointed moment at the wedding, I met Lady Leverhulme who handed me the dismantled tiara, which I stuffed hastily into my trouser pockets. I gathered up the two dressmakers who had worked on the dress and had come to arrange it for the photographs and we set off arm in arm up St James's Street. Suddenly, I realised what I had taken on and began to panic. I became convinced that I would be attacked and robbed with these priceless jewels in my pockets. I began to walk at an ever-increasing pace. It must have been a strange sight for passers-by, seeing a wedding guest, his hands stuck deep in his pockets, dragging two poor women along with him as he raced up the street, across Piccadilly and on to Farm Street and safety. Luckily, my fears were not realised and the tiara was returned safely to its owners.

Chapter Thirteen

Unusual Requests

The fashion world has probably more superstitions and idiosyncrasies than any other industry. For instance, under no circumstances did we ever fit a green ensemble on Friday 13th. Nor was anyone allowed to whistle in the workrooms in the fear that they would whistle away work. When a garment was being fitted and there had been difficulties, either in the handling of the fabric, or if the client had reservations about the style or colour or were known to be difficult, someone would place a cotton reel on the table in front of whoever had been working on the garment. A pencil, with its point towards the ceiling, was placed in the hole in the cotton reel to represent a candle and this was left until the fitting was completed. The theory was that this candle would keep away evil spirits while the fitting was taking place. A superstition that grew among the showroom staff was that when we started a new order book we must do our utmost to begin with an order for something black. It didn't matter what type of garment it was, it just needed to be black. The *vendeur* or *vendeuse* would happily take orders for materials in other colours but hold back actually writing in the order book until he or she was lucky enough to get a black garment. The idea of this was that, once blessed with a black garment, good luck would follow through the succeeding orders until the order book was full. There was also a very strong belief in the showroom that bad luck came in threes. Should one ensemble fail to please one client, the sales staff would expect to have the trouble repeated three times until the spell was broken.

Our clients were also idiosyncratic. They often had their own strange tastes and requirements that I tried my best to satisfy. At times, I think that some clients had as many whims and fancies as there are shades of material. In one spring collection, we had cut off all the suit sleeves to just below the elbow and awaited the reaction of the clients after the show. One of my most elegant clients, who managed to look as though she did nothing with her life but lie languidly on a sofa in her drawing room drinking champagne, came to place an order.

'My dear,' she said, 'I must have some suits with those short sleeves. They would be ideal for wearing at my luncheon parties. It means I won't have to change my clothes when the guests have gone and I am left with the washing up.'

I found it hard to imagine her at the sink dressed in one of my suits.

Having taken endless trouble at one particular final fitting to get the sleeves and bodice correct, I asked the client if she was satisfied.

After looking at herself in the mirror for some time, she replied, 'Oh yes, it will be quite all right when I wear it on the beach and cover it up with a white cardigan.'

Sometimes, we got some strange and unusual requests from our clients but always tried our best to accommodate. Fittings were often very enjoyable experiences and sometimes our client's eccentricities were revealed. One elegant client was having the final fitting for a silk dress and suddenly expressed a wish to walk up and down the showroom in it. This was quite a natural request, for some women like to see their new clothes in move-ment. Backwards and forwards she went, swishing her hands up and down the side of her dress, when suddenly a beam of delight came over her face.

'Ah!' she said, 'I have learned the trick.'

She must have noticed the expression on my face and said, 'You see, I only ordered the dress for the noise the mannequin girl made when she showed it to me and now I know just how to do it.'

One day, a client of mine arrived in the showroom and said that she wished to choose a silk suit. So, I gave the mannequins instructions to show all the suits we had that season. After carefully watching them, she asked for me.

'Tell me, are the silk suits made from wild silk or natural silk?'

Surprised, I asked her why she wanted to know.

'Well,' she replied, 'silk worms in captivity must be unhappy compared to silk worms that are in their natural surroundings and contented minds give contented bodies so wild worms must give better quality than silk worms in captivity.'

I could think of no answer to that.

On another occasion, a client arrived for a fitting for a new suit. The suit had a fairly straight skirt and the fitter had to pin it. When she had completed her job, I was called in to see it and comment. I was talking to both the client and the fitter when suddenly to my amazement the client disappeared. When I looked down, I saw her kneeling on the floor.

Seeing my surprised look, she said, 'Yes, the skirt will be alright. I always wear my best clothes in church on Sunday, so I must be able to kneel down and pray in it.'

At sale times, the clients, many of whom are the same size as our mannequins, try the dresses on before we alter them or let them out. One day, a jolly country woman arrived at Lachasse, made a choice and went with the fitter to a changing room. After some time, I heard laughter coming out of the room. I arrived to see both client and fitter red in the face and laughing. The client was stuck in a green wool dress and nothing could remove it. I tugged, we all pulled, but the dress would not budge. The only thing was for us to cut the stitching and let the woman out. This was done and I enquired which if any of the dresses she wanted to buy.

'Well,' she said, 'it would only be the decent thing to buy the offending dress.'

Unlikely as this seemed, it turned out to be a most successful solution and we re-christened it the 'laughing dress'.

There have been countless more examples of unusual requests from our clients. When she reached 100 years of age, Mrs Elizabeth Harvey ordered an evening dress, which she wanted to wear at the celebration dinner. The chiffon was ordered, the style was settled and the fittings took place. The day after the second fitting, she telephoned me early to say that she had been having a sleepless night about the dress and although delighted with it wanted to change the bodice.

'You see,' she said, 'if you give me a crossover bodice I could have a lower neckline and that would give me a far better bust line. This is not something to be ignored when you reach 100.'

I made several more dresses for this wonderful woman before she died aged 104. Whenever she came for her fittings, she would bring a picnic hamper and the fitters would join in her luncheon of salmon sandwiches and sherry. It delighted Mrs Harvey and I recall her saying once that it was far better to have her picnic at Lachasse as the restaurants were so noisy and crowded these days.

Catherine Walston, the American wife of Lord Walston, quite often came in for her fitting during lunchtime and she insisted on serving a picnic from her hamper complete with a check cotton tablecloth, which was spread out on the fitting room floor. Once, I was asked to make her two silk dresses, one in cream and one in red, for the Opening of Parliament. At the last fitting, Catherine insisted on having two pockets put on the side seams of each dress. When I asked her why this had to be done, she said that she often felt hungry during these ceremonies and, if the pockets were deep enough, she could hide a packet of biscuits to help her keep going.

We became quite accustomed to clients bringing in their small children to the showroom and many of these families became firm friends. But at times, we found that some of the little dears played up. One lunch time, a client brought her small son in with her along with her husband. Instead of the child sitting in fixed amazement at the clothes as most of them do, he climbed on a gold settee and then walked up and down on the white-painted windowsill, while opening and shutting the velvet curtains. Both mother and father seemed quite unaware of the child's behaviour and made no attempt to stop him.

Another tiresome small boy arrived with his mother and sat beside her while the mannequin paraded up and down.

Suddenly, ran up to the mannequin and asked at the top of his voice, in front of the other clients who had come to see the collection. 'What colour knickers are you wearing today?'

The poor mannequin was stunned and beat a hasty retreat but the mother, obviously used to this kind of behaviour, did not bat an eyelid.

In the '60s and '70s, the late Dai Llewellyn often came with his mother to one of her fittings, smartly dressed in a grey suit.

During one of these visits, he suddenly rose from the gilt chair in the fitting room, stood in front of me and said in a clear, firm voice, 'Mr Crown, my mother was voted the best dressed mother in my class at Eton. Well done. Keep it up,' and promptly sat down.

His mother, the fitters and I were dumbfounded at his remark and confidence.

Sometimes it was our clients who did not behave themselves while at Lachasse. One day, an elderly woman arrived to place an order. As soon as she entered the showroom, she told the *vendeuse* that she was not feeling well. The *vendeuse* rushed to the board room and returned with a glass of brandy. However, when the client rose from her seat to look at the dress patterns she fell over the coffee table. On picking her up, the *vendeuse* realised that she had been drinking and that her kindness had made the situation worse.

On another occasion, a client arrived to the showroom with a large bag and went directly into the loo where she stayed for some considerable time. Anxiously, I tapped on the door and asked if all was well. The door burst open and she came out much worse for wear, clutching a full sized whiskey bottle and with her large hat askew.

On seeing me, she said, 'You will never guess what I have been doing.'

'I most certainly can', I replied.

It was useless for me to help her by myself so I asked the staff to help me to get her into a car and home. Sadly, the last time I saw her she was sitting in the gutter on Charing Cross Road complete with her bottle whiskey. I heard later that she sadly died penniless.

Buying clothes at Lachasse was not inexpensive but our clothes were always worth their price because of the quality workmanship that went into each piece. My clients always had very different approaches to money and this became clear when they were settling their bills. One always paid her dress bill with cash and explained she used the egg money from her poultry farm so that her husband would not find out how much she spent on clothes. Another told me that on marrying her second husband she had an arrangement with him. He would never ask how much she paid for her clothes and she would never have to lie about the price. It seemed to be a practical arrangement. One woman always paid her dress bills with travellers' cheques. She was always making plans to go overseas and somehow the planned trips never came off for a million reasons. To cheer herself up she would buy clothes and these were always paid for using the holiday savings.

One day, a tiny woman arrived at the showroom with a large paper bag and announced that she wanted to settle her bill. She then emptied the bag on the showroom table. To the amazement of all, it was completely full of bank notes. The secretary arrived with details of her account and was asked to count out the notes to settle the bill. The rest of the money was put back in the bag. We were worried about her leaving with so much money but she was adamant that she could get home safely. She had come from the bank by public transport and was keen to return to her flat in Knightsbridge the same way.

Two weeks later, the woman came back for a fitting and I asked her if she had got home safely. She said that she had but when she reached home she gave the paper bag to her housekeeper and thought no more about it. The next day, she asked for the bag to be brought to her and the housekeeper told her that the bag had been thrown away and the rubbish men had just been. I asked her what her husband had said when she told him what had happened. She claimed that he hadn't minded and simply gave her more money to spend.

Other husbands were more concerned about how much their wives were spending at Lachasse. One husband arrived at the showroom with his wife and watched the collection being shown as we discussed what was needed and what ensembles suited Madam. The total number of ensembles she chose came to six.

'Betty, dear,' the husband said, 'you can have four.'

His wife's face fell and then a smile crept across her countenance. I quoted prices, a consultation took place between husband and wife, and four ensembles were ordered. When I wrote out the order I realised what the wife had done. She had chosen the four most expensive. After some hours the wife came back.

'I will order the other two outfits which you showed me earlier today.'

'Shall I put them all on the same account?'

'Oh, no,' said the woman, 'I will pay for the other two out of the housekeeping.'

Some of my clients wanted to look their best but didn't want other people to know how much money they were spending on their clothes. One woman remained loyal to Lachasse while living on the Isle of Man. I mailed sketches to her for her approval, the workroom prepared the garment and then I travelled to stay with her for the weekend to do the necessary fittings. She kept up a very high standard with her clothes and always dressed immaculately. One day, in her local post office, one of her friends told her how much she admired her clothes and asked where she bought them from. She was so embarrassed by her arrangement with Lachasse and didn't want to appear grand that she said that they were from the local store on the island. It was sometime later that she met the friend again, who had been searching the local store for clothes of the same standard. My client didn't give up the pretence and said that maybe the new stock hadn't arrived yet.

Sometimes clients weren't happy with their choice of clothing. I had many occasions when I had to listen patiently and try to solve their problems with the minimum of fuss. I always wanted them to be perfectly happy with their clothes. One day, a woman who was recommended to me by a friend arrived at the showroom. She told me that she needed an outfit to wear at her son's wedding. Great thought and consideration took place and she made her final choice. It was to be a topcoat in turquoise wool with a matching silk dress. Fitting times were made, the woman left and the fabrics were ordered from Paris. The day and hour of fitting arrived. The woman was ushered into the fitting room and I was busy looking after another client downstairs. A few seconds later, she rushed towards me, red in the face. Everything seemed in be in order in the workroom, so I looked at her in amazement.

'I won't have it,' she said as she came closer to me.

'Why?' I asked.

'It is not the colour I wanted. My eyes were bad when I ordered. In fact, I had been suffering from fish poisoning and it changed the colours for me.'

Nothing could be done to pacify her, so I smiled politely and ushered her out. At least it was an original excuse not to take up her commitments.

Sometimes, through no one's fault, clients need to cancel their order at short notice or we have to try and solve their often unique problems at the last minute. One morning, the mother of a bride arrived and chose a silk printed dress and jacket to wear to the wedding. Several days later, another woman arrived, looked at the clothes and selected the identical dress and jacket in the same colour and print. Two days before the planned wedding, the parents of the bride and groom met over dinner and both women revealed that they had been to Lachasse and chosen their ensembles. They took out the patterns to compare outfits and to their horror realised that they had picked the same garments. The following day, we received a hurried telephone call and the bridegroom's mother came to see us. We managed to make a second dress within two days and so helped avert a potentially embarrassing situation.

On another occasion, a maid telephoned to say that her mistress was not at all happy with her dress. She wanted to return it and to be reimbursed. I had spent a long time with the client in the fitting room and knew that there was nothing wrong with the fitter's work but I decided to take the dress back, give it to charity and refund the money. I arrived at the house with the refund in my hand and gave it to the maid. Quite some time passed before the maid, quite red in the face, handed the offending dress to me in a paper bag. Once I reached my car, I looked in the bag and could see that the dress had been worn more than once and, as the client's perfume was still strong, I could tell that it had been worn recently. We sent the dress to the cleaners at once and then on to a charity for a 'good as new' sale in aid of Cancer Research.

Several weeks later, I met a friend at a dinner party and she remarked that she was at a luncheon party when the maid called the hostess away suddenly. There seemed to be quite a lot of conversation in the hall and when the hostess returned she had completely changed her outfit. We could not work out what had happened to make her take such a sudden dislike to the dress.

It wasn't unusual for clients of Lachasse, and other businesses, to try to return their clothes, claiming that they weren't suitable after they had clearly been worn. A friend of mine who was a buyer for a large and exclusive store in the North of England told me that she had once sold an expensive fur coat to a client for a wedding. A great friend of the buyer was invited to the same wedding and, after the reception, telephoned my friend and said how good the woman looked in her new fur coat. So, she was surprised the following morning when the woman returned the coat saying that her husband didn't like it. Before taking it back, the buyer insisted on examining the coat and looked in the pockets. As she turned the pockets inside out, a shower of confetti fell out onto the counter along with a prayer book. The client went red in the face and hurriedly left the shop.

Chapter Fourteen

Famous Faces

Lachasse always attracted some of the great names from a variety of worlds, including many from the stage and screen. I helped the most fashionable stars to find the perfect garments for their appearances on stage and for glamorous events. I began to understand exactly what an actress needed to wear to steal a scene or capture the attention of the press and get everyone talking about her impeccable taste.

In the '40s and '50s, it was very fashionable for theatrical and film stars to dress with Lachasse. Zsa Zsa Gabor was so pleased with her clothes that she sent the designer a single, long-stemmed blood red rose in a large box with a covering note. We also dressed the actress Kay Kendall who arrived for her fittings full of life and vivacity and the staff soon learned exactly what she wanted. I worked closely with the American film and stage actress Dorothy Hyson, later to become Lady Anthony Quayle, and Music Hall and variety star Dorothy Ward, the pantomime actress known for her floaty chiffon dresses in soft delicate sweet pea colours.

Actress Patricia Kirkwood, famed for her appearances in musicals by Cole Porter, Noel Coward and Leonard Bernstein as well as for her fabulous legs dressed with Lachasse. Margaret Rawlings the distinguished actress was also a client of Lachasse, especially when she was at the very top of her successful career. Beryl Cooke who played in the show The Boyfriend was also a loyal client. As were the great theatrical star Evelyn Ley and Valerie Hobson, Diana Wynyard, Dulcie Gray, Yvonne Mitchell, Ambrosine Phillpotts, Dorothy Dickson and Ann Todd.

Michaela Denis who gained fame when appearing with her husband Armand in the television series Filming Wild Animals was dressed by Lachasse. She often come to the showroom from the television studio wearing heavy makeup but was always full of fun and obviously enjoyed her fittings at Lachasse.

Another great character to join Lachasse's list of clients was Angela Fox, mother of the three Fox boys, Edward, James and Robert. She was married to Robin Fox, the leading theatrical manager at the time. Angela became a great pal and whenever she ordered her clothes she would remark that she hoped her boys would approve.

When Dame Flora Robson appeared in the enormously successful play 'Black Chiffon', its author, Lesley Storm, began buying her clothes from Lachasse. It was several years later, when Miss Storm wrote the comedy, 'Roar Like a Dove', which was staged at the Phoenix Theatre in 1957, that she returned to the limelight and to Lachasse. We then had the pleasure of making more clothes for her for the many trips to Hollywood. In May 1961, the two women joined forces again in a show that Lachasse unfortunately did not dress. This time the play was called 'Time and Yellow Roses', and Miss Robson took the part of a wealthy woman.

Many Hollywood stars and directors lived close to Lachasse. When Robert Wise, director of the 'Sound of Music', came to live in London with his wife, they found a house on Brompton Square. Mrs Wise, who had been an actress, became a client at Lachasse. On one occasion, I made her a grey princess style topcoat banded with grey-black fox fur. It was a sad day when she and Robert had to leave for Hollywood in 1962 to direct Shirley MacLaine in the film 'Two For The Seesaw'.

Through Irene Lannon, who was a very loyal Lachasse client, I often met the actress Anna Neagle and her husband Herbert Wilcox, the film director. We would have long discussions about films and clothes over luncheon at a club. When Anna opened a, sadly unsuccessful, dance studio in Bond Street she threw a lavish launch party. We danced until dawn in two large studios and ate the food of the gods. She had invited stars from the stage, screen and theatre it was like a who's who of the entertainment world. The Lannons often gave summer parties in their beautiful Surrey house and on one occasion I met and talked with Lord Woolfendon in the grounds who had written the famous report on homosexuality.

I was often asked by actresses and other celebrities to design dresses for the red carpet at film première. One of the gowns that was most enjoyable to fit was for the wife of a famous actor. We started the first fitting in a jubilant mood and as each fitting progressed so did the fun. The gown was to be worn at a film première and, as we had all decided that it had to be pure white, a dark suntanned skin was the only thing that would show it to its best advantage. Fortunately, the weather was kind to Mrs Cole and by the night of the première she had acquired a very deep, golden tan. This, alongside the white dress and a Medici-blue taffeta stole became one of the most simple but dramatic effects seen at a première.

When actress Hermione Gingold returned to London after making the film 'Gigi' with Lesley Caron in America, she appeared in a show at the Piccadilly Theatre. One rainy day, I was telephoned by the television studios and asked if I would go to the theatre later that afternoon with some evening dresses that might be suitable for Miss Gingold to wear on a television show. The show was to be her first television appearance since the launch of 'Gigi' and everything had to be just right. Miss Gingold had already rejected many designers and their work as unsuitable.

The fitter and I were feeling apprehensive as we arrived by taxi with the dresses and were shown into the dressing room, which was quite small and very stuffy. It was even worse when we arrived with all the clothes which, added to her dresser and the wardrobe girl from the TV studio, only gave us enough room to move around one at a time. Slowly, we went through the dresses until we came to a one-shoulder dress in green and purple jersey with a long stole caught at the shoulder. Miss Gingold promptly threw it into the air with arms outstretched to so that it would land on her frame. The dress had other ideas and landed on top of me, engulfing and almost smothering me. At this sight, Miss Gingold broke into deep laughter. We recovered our composure, took the necessary measurements and left, scooping up all the dresses and their covers.

When the dress was ready, I was given two tickets for the showing at the television studios in Shepherds Bush. The fitter and I, very excited, were shown to seats in the front row of the audience. The set was pure white, with large Corinthian columns. At a given moment, Miss Gingold came onto the stage and floated around for some time before coming to rest in front of the audience.

'Do you all like my dress?' she enquired.

After their enthusiastic response she said, 'Well, the young man who designed it is right here, so stand up, Mr Crown, and take a bow!'

That wasn't my last experience of seeing my clothes on the stage. The impresario Peter Bridge telephoned me one day to say that he was producing a play written by Alan Ayckbourn and directed by Robert Midgley in which Robert Morley was to star. He asked whether I would take the job of designing the clothes for Joan Tetzel, who was playing Robert's wife. Joan had appeared on the London stage with Robert just after the war and this was to be her big comeback to the London theatre. I was sent a copy of the script and saw that Joan would take the part of a wealthy stockbroker's wife. After speaking to both Joan and Robert, I started on the necessary designs for her wardrobe.

When these were complete, Joan came to Lachasse with Peter Bridge and we talked about the clothes that should be worn in the different scenes. The main scene was to be a dinner party. At one end of a table, Robert and Joan would be entertaining on a grand scale and at the other end one of the table employees of Robert's business would be giving a less-lavish dinner party in a semi-detached house. My challenge was to find clothing that would be suitable for Joan's character to wear to either dinner party, as she switched to and fro during the action of the play. After much thinking and dozens of sketches, I decided on a ballet-length black taffeta dress with a wide neckline and plain sleeves. It was trimmed with black velvet and the skirt had three graduated bands of velvet going down towards the hem.

The rest of her wardrobe was fairly straightforward, apart from her outfit for her first appearance on the stage. For this, she wanted to walk on to the stage in a casual manner and give the audience the impression that nothing had changed since her last successful appearance in 'The Little Hut'. Since this last success was some years before, it was a formidable task. For this informal first entrance on stage, an actress usually wore an elegant dressing gown but Joan was determined that she should wear a dressing gown that would give her a youthful look. We couldn't find anything suitable and so had to make the dressing gown, or rather housecoat, in a glorious shade of youthful turquoise blue. It had a wide, low set collar, which was trimmed with matching satin, as were the cuffs and flapped pockets. At the first rehearsal it looked fantastic, and Joan swished across the stage like a young girl.

When the play opened at the Lyric on Shaftesbury Avenue, it got rave reviews. During its run, the country was suffering from electricity cuts and London, like everywhere else, was put on quotas and each area's supply would be cut off at certain hours. When the Lyric was in the 'off' area, Joan would come to the showroom at Lachasse and put on her stage makeup. She would then be rushed by taxi to the theatre on Shaftesbury Avenue ready for curtain-up when the lighting was restored. This went on for some time and gave us the opportunity to get to know each other. We became good friends and later she would come to me for clothes for her public appearances and photographs.

The play had an excellent run before it eventually went to the Playbill Theatre in New York in March 1971. After seeing Joan's costumes on stage, countless members of the audience asked for directions to Lachasse so that they could buy the dress for themselves. I was asked many times to make copies of Joan's ballet-length dinner dress. I made these in every colour in the paint-box but I think it always looked best in the original black taffeta and velvet.

At the same time, I was busy making a wardrobe for Cicely

Courtneidge, who was acting in 'Move Over, Mrs Markham' at the Vaudeville in the Strand. Cicely had been a friend and client for many years and I had dressed her for all her stage shows since we met in the '60s. When in 1964 she filmed 'The Wife of Knightsbridge', written by John Hallowell and directed by John Jacobs for Anglia TV, I had the pleasure of designing her whole wardrobe. Towards the end of her career, she received bad press at an opening. The following morning, before I could read the papers, she telephoned me to assure me that there was nothing to worry about. All the criticism was aimed at her and the play and not her clothes.

Cicely was great fun, though often impatient, and always brought her dear little black toy poodle with her to fittings. Fittings went on quite peacefully until he wanted to go walkies and then they would come to an abrupt halt. Whenever she went into plays, sketches or any kind of appearance, Cicely would telephone me and explain what she needed and we would make a date when I could go to her house on Charles Street with sketches and patterns. She would call for her husband, Jack Hulbert, to have a glass of sherry with us and then dismiss him so that we could get down to work I once made her the most elegant silver and blue evening dress for her Golden Wedding anniversary on 14th February 1966. The following day I got a telephone call from her. I answered apprehensively and I heard the sound of a large kiss being blown down the wires.

'Lovely, darling,' she said, 'send the bill!'

Another star who came to Lachasse was Elizabeth Welch. Thanks to her heavenly voice and ready laugh, we soon became friends. When she sang at a party for Noel Coward at the Savoy Hotel, I made her a black velvet trouser suit with bell bottom trousers and wide luxurious fox cuffs on the sleeves. This was just as the trouser look for women was about to burst onto the fashion scene and so was very daring. With her long legs, the effect was stunning and Liz returned to Lachasse many times to choose outfits for her appearances.

We also dressed Viscountess Rothermere, formerly the actress Bubbles Brook (known as such for her love of champagne) who starred as Sally in the film 'Reach for the Sky'. Her dressmaker Janet and I would go for fittings at tea time and we would sit by the fire in her Easton Square drawing room and the staff were told to give us whatever refreshments we requested. On one occasion, I made a black velvet and emerald satin dress for her to wear at a reception at the Savoy Hotel.

The actress, Dulcie Gray was a client at Lachasse for many years and came originally for clothes to be made for her television work. Dulcie was one of the kindest people in show business and always came to the showroom with her husband, Michael Denison. The three of us would look at the clothes, discuss the plays and shows and then arrive at a final decision about what would be suitable. On one occasion, I had the pleasure of designing Dulcie's wardrobe for a murder play. In all, she had six ensembles, which had to cover from breakfast time to bedtime. She had a housecoat in pink cloque, which she liked so much that when she was the subject of 'This Is Your Life' she chose to wear it in the studio.

For many years, Mrs Poulson came to Lachasse to buy clothes with her husband, who would help her make the final choice. She liked tailored clothes in conservative colours. It was hard to believe that her husband was at the centre of a huge storm in English political life in 1972. I remember that on the last few occasions that Mrs Poulson came to see the collection, she seemed to find it difficult to concentrate or to make a final decision and I remember remarking to some of the showroom staff that she seemed pre-occupied. She never showed any of the terrible emotion, which must have been welling up inside her. She remained outwardly calm while her life crashed around her.

Amongst the many celebrities who were clients at Lachasse was the socialite Diana Barnato Walker, daughter of millionaire racing driver Woolf 'Babe' Barnato and granddaughter of a South African diamond millionaire. She joined the ATA (Air Transport Auxiliary) in 1941 to deliver newly-built aircrafts to airfields all over southern England. By the age of 22, she had delivered 240 Spitfires and many other aircrafts and had risked her life countless times. It was always hard to believe that this small, elegant woman standing for her fitting in the Lachasse showroom had done such brave work during the war and in 1963 she became the first British woman to break the sound barrier.

One day whilst Diana was in the fitting room, concealed behind a screen, two menacing looking men suddenly appeared in the showroom and demanded money. Diana left her fitter and told the thugs that this was a woman's dress shop, that there was no cash on the premises and that they should leave. Her coolness and courage left me speechless. She somehow walked them to the door and got them out onto the street before returning to her fitting.

Lachasse clients were from many different worlds and I often found myself dressing musicians. From the 1960s, Marguerite Wolff, the concert pianist, became a regular client of Lachasse. For her many trips abroad for the Foreign Office, she required a full wardrobe and a very special dress for each of her perform-ances. When she was awarded an OBE for services to the country and work overseas, I designed a pink wool suit trimmed with palma violet, which enhanced her tiny frame beautifully.

One late afternoon, the doorbell rang at Lachasse and I found a young man with his girlfriend waiting on the step. They were interested in buying hats for the woman. These had to be small, exotic and easy to keep on the head. They chose several hats and left in a hurry. Quite often over the next few weeks they would return for the same purpose. It was not until later that I realise that the man was in the band Def Leopard and that his American girlfriend always wore a different hat at each of his performances as a good luck charm.

I was often asked to make special outfits for well-known figures to wear at public functions. Lachasse dressed many women from the political world as they found that our type of clothing fitted into their wardrobe and way of life. When Mrs Mallinson became Mayor of Westminster in 1986, she bought many pieces for her wardrobe from Lachasse and during her year in office I met with her many times. Both Mrs Mallinson and the clothes had great success during her mayoral year.

Two dresses that gave the wearer great publicity were made

for Baroness Betty Boothroyd, when she was speaker in the House of Commons. During her reign as speaker, we were privileged to make quite a number of garments for her own wardrobe and her very busy professional life. For a major television interview, we once made her a scarlet red re-embroidered lace cocktail dress. It was an instant success and gained both its wearer and Lachasse a great deal of praise around the world.

Another of her dresses that won press admiration for Baroness Boothroyd was a silver *lamé* and chiffon evening gown called 'Silver Dollar', which she chose to wear at a gala evening for the media. This dress held its own against fierce competition from starlets from the stage, film and television. We also made a jersey dinner dress for Lady Boothroyd called 'Mischief'. I had the pleasure of making several outfits for Baroness Thatcher including, in 2003, a petrol blue pure silk and cashmere coat frock for a service held at Westminster Abbey to mark the fiftieth anniversary of the Queen's coronation.

Chapter Fifteen

Social Life

Having a job such as mine was rather like being on stage. I was on duty the whole time and no matter where I went, for a drink with a few friends, to a cocktail party or even to a restaurant for a meal, I would often bump into one of my many clients. They always expected me to be immaculately dressed, whatever the circumstances, and I took a great deal of pride in my appearance. I had to make sure that my own wardrobe was constantly in good order and ready for any invitations I received. When I was teaching four nights a week at St Martin's School of Art, I thought nothing of popping into a cocktail party en route to the evening class or dashing home after teaching, changing quickly and joining a party for supper after a show. Luckily, living in Belgravia saved me a lot of travelling time.

Being a man in a trade where there is a predominance of women, I received a great many invitations to social events. When American *débutantes* arrived in London to do a continental tour in the '60s and '70s, I was often asked to show some of the girls around town by Mrs Rennie O'Mahoney, who ran a school for *débutantes* on Charles Street. What a week I had during their visits each summer. We went to the theatre and to two or three parties each night. I often returned home at dawn just in time for me to get ready for a day at Lachasse. After a busy day at work, I would go out again. On and on we went, tirelessly. I got to know exactly how much sleep and rest my body needed.

I think that one of the greatest compliments I ever had was from one of my girls at Lachasse when she said, 'The wonderful thing about you is that you never look tired, and are always full of energy.'

London in the '50s and '60s was exciting and I made the most of every minute. The restaurant Le Caprice in Arlington House, run by Mario Gallati, was the meeting place to be seen at, especially after the first night at the theatre, and I dined there frequently. Mario, a small and very polite Italian man greeted you as you arrived and when a table was ready he would guide you to it. As you wound your way past the other guests, celebrities of every type could be seen. On occasions, I saw Doris Day, Margot Fontaine, Hayley Mills, Arthur Askey and Lady Docker. The food was magnificent and I always ended my meal with fried ice cream, a pancake lightly fried but filled with dark chocolate ice cream.

From my first tentative years in London, one of my major interests was in theatrical costume. Whenever I watched a play, I was usually focusing on the costumes and trying to work out who designed them and how they were made. In October 1972, I joined a party to see the first night of the play 'The Day after the Fair', written by Frank Harvey. It starred Deborah Kerr and Avice Landon and the period costumes were delightful. During the interval, I told my hostess, Mrs Joyce Hyde, about my interest in costume. She was a great friend of Avice and we soon were all invited backstage after the show to meet the glamorous star. After the final curtain, we all crowded into Avice's dressing room and enjoyed a drink with her and her husband, Bruno. I was examining the dresses Avice had worn, when the door opened and Deborah Kerr came in to say goodnight. Seeing my interest in the clothes, she joined in the technical conversation on making clothes for the cinema and stage. It was a great treat for me to have such a conversation with two such distinguished ladies of stage and screen.

While working in the fashion world, I met many distinguished artists. At one dinner party, I met Kathleen Nevinson, wife of the late CRW Nevinson, the famous war artist. After the meal, Kathleen asked if I had any of her late husband's work. I replied that I had no spare cash for artwork. Several days later, I arrived home to find a parcel on my doorstep. Inside was one of CRW Nevinson's studies that Kathleen had sent me as a Christmas present.

Photography became another of my interests and this led me into a new sphere in my social life. In 1964, I discovered the work of the husband and wife team, Una Mary and Archie Parker. They had photographed the Queen, Prince Philip and the young members of the royal family and when I met the couple they were expanding their photographic business.

A good friend of Una Mary's was Christine Dickie, one of the head organisers at Winkfield Place, Windsor Forest. This beautiful house was used by the Constance Spry School for teaching future hostesses how to run a household, entertain and make flower arrangements. Christine frequently invited friends and celebrities to dine at Winkfield as her guests. The students would serve the drinks, cook and serve the meal and make glorious floral arrangements. When I dined there in 1967, the guests included Norman Hartnell and Madame Vernier, one of London's leading milliners. Madame Vernier herself gave the most wonderful dinner parties in her studio flat near Marble Arch, where she gathered together a most interesting array of people – authors, sculptors, people from the theatre and fashion worlds and a few musical and legal celebrities. With her sharp, intelligent conversation, she drew ideas from us all. When it was time to leave one had the satisfaction of knowing that one's mind had been as well sustained as one's stomach.

On one occasion in 1976, Una Mary invited me to a charity performance at the Phoenix Theatre. The play was 'The Pleasure of his Company' by Samuel Taylor and starred Douglas Fairbanks Jr, Dinah Sheridan, David Langton and Wilfred Hyde White. Dinah had been a client at Lachasse during her marriage to John Davis of J Arthur Rank fame. She came to see me one day and we soon became good friends. I designed some clothes for a trip she was taking to the Far East, including a long, black, slinky dinner dress called 'Phaedra'. She loved this dress and, when I asked her to be one of my guests at a dinner at the Merchant Taylors' Hall in the city, she asked me what I would like her to wear.

'Phaedra,' I answered.

Although it was several years since the dress had been made, and the occasion was a very glittering and fashionable one, Dinah stole the show just as she did when we first met.

Because of my working hours, I usually had to refuse invitations to luncheon parties but I always made time for literary luncheons organised by Miss Christina Foyle. Miss Foyle was surely one of the busiest women in Britain in her day but she always seemed outwardly serene and unmoved by the clock.

It was in April 1959 when Miss Foyle first invited me to be a guest at the top table after I had made her several ensembles. It was an exciting occasion as the guest of honour was Mrs Eleanor Roosevelt, who was in London to celebrate the publication of her autobiography, 'On My Own'. It was at this luncheon that I also met Dame Sybil Thorndyke and Lady Churchill. Dame Sybil had just returned from one of her trips abroad and was on sparkling form. Over the years, I was often invited to be a guest at the top table. In 1978, I was lucky enough to join HRH The Prince Philip, Duke of Edinburgh, to celebrate the publication of the book 'The Environmental Revolution'.

At later Foyle's luncheons, I was introduced to many well known figures. I had the pleasure of meeting the wife of Ranjit S Pandit, who immediately struck me as being one of the world's most humane and far-seeing women. I met many authors, including Malcolm Muggeridge, author of 'Chronicles of Wasted Time', Joy Adamson, the author of 'Born Free', J B Priestley, who was given a luncheon to launch his book 'Man and Time' and Mary Quant when she launched her book 'Quant by Quant'. On other occasions, I found myself sitting next to influential people from the political world such as Lord and Lady Attlee, Mrs Hugh Gaitskell, Lady Eccles and Mrs Peter Thornycroft and many well known figures including the astronomer, Patrick Moore, scientist Dr Magnus Pyke, mountaineer Chris Bonington, broadcaster Michael Parkinson and actor Sir John Gielgud.

I was introduced to people who would become great friends. Among these were Ursula Bloom, the novelist, and her husband Commander Gower Robinson. Our friendship was cemented

when Ursula and I discovered that she and I were both chris-
tened at the same font, at St Peter's Church, Swaffham, Norfolk,
making us, we decided, relations by baptism. Ursula was a pro-
lific writer and had written hundreds of books by the time we
met. Whenever she published a new book, I was given a signed
copy and once even dedicated one to my mother and myself. Not
only was she a great writer but also a keen needlewoman and
embroidered my monogram on all my linens.

Ursula was a great supporter of many charities with which I
was involved but her kindness became most valuable to me
personally in 1975. It was then that the house where I was living
was threatened with demolition, along with its neighbours. The
Pont Street Defence Group was formed with the help of Mr and
Mrs Edmund van Moppes with the aim of preventing the Pont
Street 'Dutch' houses from being razed to the ground and
replaced by a modern block of flats with an underground car
park. Everyone of note who had connections with Chelsea and
Knightsbridge, including Sir John Betjeman and Spike Milligan,
rallied behind us and the battle raged for many years. With the
support of the media and the ceaseless efforts of our committee,
headed by the van Moppes and myself, we eventually won and
in 1977 managed to get the houses listed Grade II. Although
from the outside, five of the houses remained intact, inside they
were made into more modern flats. The sixth house, in which I
live, is luckily on a different elevation and has been left the same
both inside and out.

One evening, when I was at a rare loose end, I was invited to
a Dance Studio as the guest of one of my clients. I arrived and as
soon as the door was opened, I realised that I had made a great
mistake in accepting the invitation. The corridor to the studio
was full of theatrical relics from the '30s, which fought to be
seen amidst souvenirs from trips abroad and plaster masks
obviously won at fun fairs. The walls displayed portraits of oily-
looking young men in rather absurd attire and strangely dressed
women. Their heads stuck out from the mountains of spangled
tulle and reminded me of a particular type of teacosie that was
popular in the mid '30s. After walking down the long corridor, I

entered a large studio where people were sitting around talking. A record-player was blaring out tunes from the '40s and '50s and a few elderly women were being guided around the dance floor by over-dressed and dubious-looking young men. There was a small bar in the corner where my hostess led me and gave me a much-needed glass of champagne.

I stood there firmly for some time, swigging champagne and watching the other guests being pushed, shoved or thrown around the floor by the male escorts. It was a pitiful sight, seeing these tired, over-painted women trying to keep up with their very much younger partners. Suddenly, I was conscious of a woman by my side who looked rather different from the rest. She was dressed in a long dress of almond pink wild silk and sitting amid her neatly-dressed grey hair was a small paste tiara. We began to speak and she asked me why I was not dancing. Feeling trapped, I put my glass down and asked her formally for the next dance.

After some more polite conversation, I asked her if she came to the studio very often.

'Yes,' she replied, 'I do almost every day.'

'Oh,' I said, 'are you going in for an award for ballroom dancing?'

'No, no,' she replied, 'I am the cloakroom attendant and this is my night off!'

I did not accept any more invitations for this form of entertainment. I learned my lesson and, from then on, preferred to keep to my usual set of friends. One of them, known as one of the kindest and most generous host in Chelsea was David, known as Baron Heneage. He gave the most wonderful parties at Christmas time, when the large double drawing-room would be ablaze with a log fire at each end and candlelight from the chandeliers. There would always be a buffet supper of superb quality and a mixed gathering of people from the arts and political worlds would be invited to join his own wide circle of friends. Together, we drank and danced in the warm, mellow light or listened to a piano recital of David's own compositions.

When David telephoned one day to say that he would like to

Special Clients and Special Creations

HM The Queen with Mrs Henry Clive
wearing her High Sheriff Suit specially designed by PLC

Baroness Betty Boothroyd of Sandwell PC OM
© *Terry Moore*

Marguerite Wolff OBE
© *Edward Lloyd*

Charity Work

With HRH The Princess Margaret
at the Berkeley Hotel

With HRH Prince Michael of Kent
at IHC Hotel

With HRH the Duchess of Kent
at Syon House

With HRH Princess Alexandra
at Imperial College © *P.E. Holland*

Charity Work

With Dame Norma Major DBE
at Drapers' Hall

With HRH Princess Alexandra
at Drapers' Hall

At Castle Howard judging a students' fashion competition

With Rolf Harris at Knightsbridge Barracks © *Edward Lloyd*

Social Life

With friends Neil Durden-Smith,
Judith Chalmers, Jean Jaffa, Ronnie Corbert,
and Pauline Johnston at the
Annenberg Theatre © *George Boyne*

With friends at Henley

PLC at polo Smith's Lawn

In fancy dress at a Ball in the Mansion House

Special Clients and Special Creations

Peter's Muse: Baroness Wilcox of Plymouth © National Magazine Co.

HRH The Princess of Wales with Countess Rothermere wearing
PLC's special evening dress in velvet, satin and lace

Fashion Shows

Thunder
and Lightning

Thurloe Place

Chatsworth
© *Ian Fraser-Martin*

Special Occasions

With HRH The Princess Royal
at the Guildhall © *P.E. Holland*

At Tallow Chandlers Hall – The Guild of Freemen © *P.E. Holland*

Lord Mayor Show – Butchers' Hall
© *P.E. Holland*

OBE Ceremony at Buckingham Palace © *Charles Green*

Wearing 'the' suit
From Julia Robson – *The Telegraph*

"The gentlemen showed the boys a thing or two (at Ascot)
Designer Peter Lewis-Crown's sharp, white waistcoat with pinstripe tails also oozed class.
Simply by adhering to the rules of formal dress, they showed the young 'uns how it's done."

throw a small dinner party and invite my close friends, Mrs Joan Rundel Mainwaring and the Duchess of Argyll, I was happy to accept the invitation. We settled on a date in April and after I finished lecturing at St Martin's School of Art, I took a taxi and got to his home at 16 The Boltons at 8pm. Joan had already arrived and was sitting in David's study. I had just been handed a drink when the doorbell rang and the Duchess of Argyll was shown into the room. Dressed in black chiffon, she looked, as always, cool, elegant and beautiful and she immediately began to tell us about the latest addition to her family – a black toy poodle. After we had dined and the time came for us to leave, we shared a car and exchanged stories of David's kindness to us all. We could never have predicted that a few years later he would tragically take his own life in his new Belgravia home after having never recovered from moving from The Boltons, which seemed for him to be the end of an era. He was one of the last of the great eccentrics and his death left a gap in the lives of his many friends.

I have been lucky enough to make many great friends and they have often shared my love of fashion. For many years, I spent Sunday evenings with Kenneth and Pepita Burness. Pepita loved her clothes and, with her dark Latin colouring, she wore clothes of the most attractive sunshine colours on her tiny neat figure. I would arrive with my patterns and sketches and settle down in their elegant drawing room with a gin and tonic and discuss her wardrobe. Her sister, the actress Patricia Medina, who later married Joseph Cotten, often stayed with Kenneth and Pepita and our conversations focused on fashion, films and travel. I became part of their family as their son Christopher and daughter Jenny grew up. When Jenny came of age, she became a client at Lachasse and when she married I had the pleasure of making her trousseaux.

In the 1960s, I was invited to spend many New Year's Eves with the artist Irma Hardy at her house in South Kensington and it was there that I met many people from the opera and ballet world. Anita Hookham, the mother of Margot Fontayne, was a regular guest. Eva Turner, the great opera singer, would often be there and we discussed cooking, which was of mutual interest to us. She once sent me her delicious recipe for Lancashire Hot Pot.

On several occasions over the years, Paul Cheffins invited Eva Gardiner, several mutual friends and myself to dine on board 'The Iris'. This was a boat used in the evacuation of Dunkirk and bought by Thames Television for a hospitality boat and moored at Teddington Lock. It was at one of these dinner parties that I first met the impresario Harold Fielding and his secretary and he invited me to the first night of his new musical.

My early days at Chelsea always became fresh in my mind again when I visited Lady Munnings, widow of the painter Sir Alfred, at her town house in Chelsea Park Gardens. We were great friends and she often called on me to be host for her at parties. She lived surrounded by her husband's paintings and with her famous dog, Black Knight. When the dog died, Violet had him stuffed and would carry him affectionately in her arms. Later, she had a large brown dog called Toby. Violet claimed that she had taught Toby to sing, so at one of my parties I requested a song. Violet sang a few notes herself and Toby raised his head and uttered a soulful whine. This was the prelude to an extended duet until I realised the guests had had enough and produced some chocolate drops for Toby and a glass of champagne for Violet in gratitude for the effort and a return to peace and quiet. Violet was always kind to me and whenever we met, either at a Foyle's luncheon or some other gathering, plans would be made for a celebration of some kind. She kept an estate in the country, which housed many of Sir Alfred's finest works, but her real enjoyment was her home in Chelsea, with the friends she had gathered around her throughout her life.

At one party I attended, I met Princess Zouina Banhalla and her husband, Basil Hope Gibson and we soon became friends. Zouina held a great many parties and, as her social circle was wide, she always invited the most fascinating people. At one of Zouina's supper parties, I met the actor Victor Spinetti. He was Welsh by birth but Italian by nature name and kept us fascinated by his stories of Hollywood. He was a friend of John Lennon and

Yoko Ono and told a wonderful story about one occasion when John Lennon was entertaining him in his flat in New York. John suddenly asked Victor if he had his passport on him and, on finding that he did, sent out for flight tickets. A car was waiting at the door of the apartment building and they were driven to Kennedy Airport. On arrival, John informed Victor that they were off to Marrakesh, as Victor had remarked that he was feeling cold. Within hours, they were in warm sunshine but with very little cash on them. Presumably their credit cards or John's celebrity took care of them financially. Victor always kept us amused until the early hours, even though he had often already performed in two shows at Victoria Place that day when he starred in a brilliant play about the newspaper world called 'Windy City'.

It was at the committee meeting for the Spring Ball where I met Pam Weisweiller, the wife of Rudi. At the time they were living in Hillsleigh Road, off Notting Hill. Rudi had inherited the family estate and castle near Salzberg called Schloss Wimsbach, which had been taken over by the SS during the Second World War. In 1998, to celebrate their golden wedding anniversary, they decided to give a period ball at the castle and invited many guests from London. Accommodation was well planned. Some guests stayed in hotels in the villages around but we were all given a chance to spend a few days in the castle. The sun shone and the reception was held in a beautiful meadow, which added romance to the period costumes we all wore. It was a wonderful event and, from the moment the planes landed in Salzberg, the guests were kept entertained. We were given a tour of the castle, including the attic, which stretched around the whole castle and was filled with treasures.

I had many chances to escape London and visit friends who lived in the country. This was always a wonderful opportunity for me to relax away from Lachasse. Once a year, my friends living in Castle Keep, Reigate gave a large party. If the weather was fine, it was held in a marquee in their beautiful garden, which was surrounded by a moat overhung with trees and home to a large duck population. These were close friends of long standing so, whenever these parties were held, I was expected to help and to act as co-host.

On several occasions, a motor coach was organised to bring parties for friends and acquaintances up from Brighton. Many of these guests had theatrical connections and had moved to Brighton to enjoy the sea breezes and relaxed social life. One such person among this group was Douglas Byng, known to all as Douggie. By the time I met him, he was in his nineties but full of life and energy. He was always impeccably dressed and gave the air of being a true English gentleman. It was difficult to believe that he had been one of the most elegant and famous female impersonators of his day, with long clinging dresses and jewels. He had a long career on the stage. He joined the cast of 'The Periodicals at the Palacette' in Hastings in July 1914 and during the two years that followed toured the country in 'The Girl in a Taxi'. He worked as an understudy at the Gaiety Theatre in September 1916 and later appeared in pantomime as well as in an endless list of theatrical productions.

For many years in the '60s, I was a frequent guest of John and Lorna Stanners in Boscastle on the north Cornish coast. They lived in a house with a terraced garden, rather like an oriental tea garden, on a hillside overlooking the river Jordan as it flowed into the Atlantic at Boscastle Bay. John, who once worked for the Hudson Bay Company and had lived many years inside the Arctic Circle, came to live in Boscastle when he retired. Quite often, I would travel down by train at weekends and, on arriving late, would be given supper on a tray in John's study. Their house was so full of memories of the Arctic and Eskimo carvings that it resembled a small museum. When they moved from Boscastle to a little fisherman's cottage called Little Fursewain, near Jamaica Inn, miles away from civilization, I very much doubted their wisdom. However, in no time the little house, in its own grounds with its own rickety bridge and fishing rights, became a gem and a fitting background for their treasures.

One weekend, Lorna announced that she had met someone that she knew I would like and had invited her to lunch that Sunday. Though I was not too thrilled at having a stranger added to our little circle, my doubts disappeared when Bunty Kitson arrived. She was a lively and delightful woman with golden blonde curls falling onto her shoulders and lived alone in a house that was once a cowshed, surrounded by a beautiful garden that she had created from nothing.

After this first meeting, we soon became friends and on several occasions I went to stay with her. This was always an adventure as her house could be unpredictable. On one of my visits, the water level fell below the line necessary to work the pump, which supplied the house with water. Undaunted, Bunty, organised an emergency water supply and told me that the bathroom had, for the time being, moved to the garden. On the first morning, wearing my dressing gown and slippers and armed with a toothbrush and other essentials, I was ushered into the garden. There, behind a hedge, stood an old fashioned hip bath. Large jugs and cans of rainwater stood on a table and Bunty, cheerful as ever, started to fill the bath. Thank heavens that the sun shone as I soaped myself down, cosseted by the additional luxury of Elizabeth Arden 'Blue Grass' bath essence.

Bunty later went to live in the East Wing of Antony House, Torpoint, Cornwall but kept her little cottage. The last time I stayed with Bunty in the grand house, we rose at dawn and wandered across the lawn picking fresh mushrooms for breakfast. Often, Lorna Stanners joined us to visit some of the historic houses in the area, places like Trerice, Pencarrow, Cotele and Lanhydroch with its banks of rhododendrons. While we visited these sights, John spent hours visiting local antique shops and auction rooms. The memories of those happy days remain with me, despite the passing of the years.

Chapter Sixteen

Personality

It became obvious in the late '50s that I needed to adopt a more showman-like attitude to my business life. I was very happy working in Lachasse but my work began to take me outside of the fitting room. I slowly began to accept invitations from all over the country and to give speeches and lectures and be interviewed on television and radio.

After working a long day at Lachasse, I often rushed to the station with a mannequin and a large part of the collection packed into suitcases and hat boxes. Once on the train, I changed in the toilet and was ready to be the guest of honour at a dinner and then give a lecture or speech afterwards. While the mannequin showed the clothes to the audience, I gave a detailed description of the fabrics and styles and explained the creation of the collection as a whole. Usually, an informal gathering followed and then it was a rush to pack the clothes away before I headed for bed. I only ever managed a few hours sleep before racing to catch the first train back to London the next morning.

My journeys across the country on these trips were not without incident. On one occasion, I was changing in the toilet on the way to an engagement, while the train rocked from side to side. Suddenly, the bolt on the door jerked back and the door flew open, much to the surprise of an anxious traveller who found me virtually naked and ready to put on my black jacket and bow tie.

For several years in the early '60s, I travelled to these events with Bridget, a house mannequin. She looked just like Grace Kelly and was cool on stage but great fun when off duty. On one occasion, Bridget, and I were running late and almost missed our train. We ran across the platform, dragging the cases of clothes and hats behind us, and caught it with seconds to spare. So that she would be ready for the show on our arrival, Bridget decided to fix her makeup on the train. It was a hazardous endeavour as she fixed her eyelashes with tweezers in one hand and a mirror in the other as the train jolted to and fro. After some considerable time, the job was completed and the makeup finished to her satisfaction. It was only then that we realised that this natural operation to Bridget had aroused a great deal of interest from the other passengers in our compartment. I think they thought we were some kind of circus act preparing for a performance.

Once, when I was travelling to Hengrave Hall in Sussex to deliver a speech in aid of the Duke of Edinburgh's Award Scheme, we actually did miss the train. Imagining all the problems this could cause, I dashed to the telephone and rang the organiser, Mother Paul, who took the news in her stride and arranged for a car to meet us from the next train. When we did catch that train we unexpectedly met the charming Mrs Harry Wragg, wife of the famous jockey and trainer, who invited us to join her and share the goodies she had just bought at Fortnum & Mason. We were met as arranged and driven at speed to Hengrave Hall, then a school but once the resting place of Catherine Parr on her way to London to marry Henry VIII. It was dark when we arrived and, when the great carved wooden door opened, we were greeted by a nun carrying a lighted candle. We were shown to the room where the lecture was to be given, ate a hasty meal and quickly sorted out the clothes we had brought. Moments later, the room filled with students and Mother Paul sat in the midst of them, looking rather like a shepherd amongst her flock.

I began my lecture and Bridget showed the clothes. We were given refreshments and the questions began. The audience asked questions about everything and they went on and on. It was late in the evening when the show finally ended. Bridget went to her room and I was led across the courtyard by a nun to a barn where the upper storey had been converted into a suite for male visitors with all modern amenities, including a shell-pink bath.

Another nun brought me a hot drink and biscuits before I turned in, exhausted by the day's events.

Next morning, I was woken by Mother Paul who brought me a flask of tea and more biscuits. Then my bath was run but not before Mother Paul had taken care of a large spider, saying that it was one of God's creatures and should be allowed to roam the outside world. I dressed hurriedly and met Bridget in the library, where we were given breakfast. The woman responsible for the grounds and the farm kept us company. During breakfast, she told us about the history of the house. As I looked out of the window and down the long walk, where the nuns walked in pairs among the yew trees, I could easily imagine the days she was describing.

When breakfast was over, we returned to the lecture room for yet another session and more questions. Mother Paul then took us for a guided tour around the Hall and grounds and told us that with their farm they were more or less self-sufficient. By the side of the little church, I spotted a greengage tree and was told that this was the first of its kind to be brought to this country by the Gage family, who owned the Hall and gave the fruit its name. By the side of the church was a large pond, kept fully stocked with fish. The journey back to London on the Saturday seemed very dull after such an eventful time.

In 1963, I was invited to speak at a very different event. I was invited to speak at the Sesame Imperial Club at the Literary Luncheon for the Men and Women of Today Club. Knowing the calibre of speakers, I agreed to do so with some reservation. Among those I knew had spoken there in the past were Lord and Lady Longford, Ursula Bloom, Flora Sandstrom, Russell Braddon, Dulcie Gray and Denise Robyns. It was the custom for Louise to give each speaker a gift. My speech seemed to go very well and I sat down to a good round of applause but there was no gift for me. The two other speakers finished their speeches and little wrapped boxes were handed to them.

My heart sank, until Louise in her charming way said, 'You know, Peter dear, I always give each speaker a little gift? Well, I have one for you but you must come to my flat to fetch it.'

It was several weeks later when I arrived for dinner at Louise's flat and met the other guests, some of whom were mutual friends. Dinner was served, we went into the drawing room for coffee and there was still no sign of the promised gift. Coffee was served in the most enchanting little hand-painted demi-tasse coffee cups and I remarked on how much I liked them.

Louise looked up, smiled and said, 'I have been waiting to hear you say that you liked something in my flat and at last you have. When we have finished coffee, the cups will be washed and packed up with the rest of the set for you to take home.'

She was a remarkable woman and this was an inventive way to find a gift that I would treasure for the rest of my life.

Other lectures didn't end so well and some proved to be extremely hard work. One such challenging experience was at the Kensington Close Hotel, in 1975, when I was invited by the Euro-Japanese Exchange Foundation to speak to a group of clothing manufacturers from Tokyo. When I had finished my talk, the group refused to let us leave, to stop for coffee or even take a short rest. Questions were fired at me like cannon balls, with a separate volley for the poor mannequin. Whenever I sat down, someone in the audience stood up, bowed, presented me with a gift and asked more questions about the clothes, the fashion trade in England or about my life. It was clear that they wanted to get their money's worth. Questions were asked until the organiser, seeing my state of exhaustion, told me to stand, bow, thank them and make a run for the door. I left the clothes and hats behind and had to ask the hotel staff to retrieve them as I couldn't face going back in the room. Several days later, I had a long and detailed thank you letter, plus my fee, which I truly felt I had more than earned.

Many of these shows were memorable but I think the greatest, and certainly the largest, was at Bedford Modern School in 1978 as part of the Bedfordshire Women's Institute Diamond Jubilee celebrations. Over five hundred people bought tickets and the fashion show and lecture were to be the focal point of the evening. We left London in a large motor coach as usual, with the staff and mannequins seated on one side and the collection on the other side of the aisle. Hats were boxed and piled high on the back seats. Clothes brushes, pins, cotton and mirrors filled the bus. Nothing was left to chance. On arrival, the clothes were sorted and checked and we relaxed over a delicious buffet supper.

Then, it was action time. When makeup was finished, clothes examined, jewellery and hats allotted, the chairwoman led me out through a small door onto the stage, followed by four mannequins. Lights blazed and, as I peered into the auditorium, I could see nothing but women from floor to ceiling. There was no retreating and so, after the introductions, I plunged into my lecture. A break for coffee and biscuits was scheduled but I had scarcely left the stage before a harassed-looking lady knocked on the door of my dressing room and demanded that I return to the stage as the audience were impatient for more. So, back we went and it was not until the whole collection of ninety ensembles had been shown and discussed that I was able to escape, to deafening applause and with beautiful bouquets for the mannequins. It was an unforgettable evening and as we boarded the bus for home some of the audience was still firing questions at us.

I was often asked to give lectures to people within the clothing industry. In October 1964, I was invited to speak to the Oxford University Design Society at Somerville College. When we arrived, the mannequin, Bridget, and I climbed a narrow wooden staircase to the lecture room, which luckily had a small room leading off it that could be used as a changing room. A great interest was shown in the design and construction of the garments and the lecture was based more on the geometry of cutting than the inspiration of design. The questions that followed made me keenly aware that academics can also have a strong feeling for art.

On many occasions, I spoke to groups of people in the textile industry and, in December 1973 was invited by the Linen Industry Research Association to speak to their members at Lisburn in Northern Ireland. This was the beginning of a close association and I was later asked by HAC Todd and Christopher French-Mullen to advise on weaves, colours and design. Eighteen months of research work on new types of fabric for fashion and furnishings followed, culminating in an exhibition at the Lambeg Research Institute. Princess Margaret and the Earl of Snowdon were there to see the final product – a tunic dress and collarless duster coat in ivory linen blend, trimmed with ivory satin. The fabric we produced was subsequently mixed with glass filaments to make it flame-proof and it was used as curtains in aeroplanes and hotels.

I returned to Lambeg to give lectures many times over the years and always stayed at the Culloden Hotel on the south side of Belfast Lough. Beautifully decorated and with spectacular views from its hundred-foot tower, it was the perfect hotel in which to rest after the hectic days spent at the Institute. On one of these visits, Chris French-Mullen suggested that he take me to meet a rather special woman who had her own mills at Rostrevor. Gerd Hay Edie, a Norwegian by birth, had settled in Northern Ireland in a house at the foot of the Mountains of Mourne. It was mutual admiration from the start and a never-to-be-forgotten first visit. It seemed strange that in the remote Irish countryside we were planning and designing fabrics and colours that women would wear in cities all over the world.

I began my broadcasting career early in the '60s, after a chance meeting with the producer George Angell at a Foyle's luncheon. He suggested that Nancy Wise should interview me and I was offered the choice of recording at the BBC in Langham Place or at my flat in Knightsbridge. I opted for the latter as I thought I would feel more comfortable in my own home. I had nothing to worry about because as soon as Nancy arrived at my flat she put me at my ease. We chatted freely about my career and the fashion industry in general and before I knew it the interview was over.

I was told that the interview would be broadcast on Mid Week and that I would be paid five guineas. I was both thrilled and terrified at the prospect and told my family and some friends to listen. When the day came, I had half of Great Britain tuned in to hear my interview. The programme began and ended with no sound of my voice. I telephoned Nancy who explained that the interview would be used in a future edition as at the last minute they had had to include subjects with more news value than mine. I tried to explain this to family, friends and clients but got a rather cool reception. Luck was with me, however, as the following week the interview went out and I received a fan club response, both at home and at Lachasse.

I was launched on my media career and soon received more interview requests. I was interviewed next by Fiona Spring-Rice for Anglia TV and then, after an article in a Norfolk newspaper, by Jean Goodman for BBC TV in Norwich. Jean interviewed me first on my life story and later filmed several fashion spectaculars on the current collections. For each of these, I dashed to Norwich with two mannequins for the filming and returned to London in time to teach at St Martin's School of Art in the evening. On one occasion, the filming went on longer than expected and I had to dash to Norwich station wearing the thick makeup that was used in television studios at the time. I leapt on to the train and found a compartment with only one man sitting in it. He watched in amazement as I produced a towel and began scrubbing at my face. Understanding and relief became evident as I explained why I was wearing full makeup at 6pm.

Jean Goodman and I often worked together and, in 1965, I did another piece for television called 'Don't change in the train', based on fashions suitable for wearing away from home. It went out on the Light Programme on BBC Radio and was once again successful. I did several more sound broadcasts with Nancy Wise in London and then Jean came up with the idea of 'Mystery Man,' where viewers had to guess my occupation based on a series of clues. For this, I was filmed on my way to work. I bought my daily carnation at Moyses Stevens on Berkeley Square and then entered the little black and white door to Lachasse, which had its name blanked out.

The presenter asked, 'Who was this man and what was he doing?'

Later, the film showed my work inside the showroom, illustrating a typical scene inside a couture house. This short film was an excellent introduction into life in the fashion industry for a wide audience across the country.

Chapter Seventeen

Textiles

I had always been interested in textiles, from my childhood days spent making fancy goods to sell in my mother's shop in Hunstanton to the frantic days spent finding the perfect fabric from which to build a collection at Lachasse. I developed an expertise in textiles and an enthusiasm that has never left me. In particular, I always had an interest in designing costumes for the theatre and learned about the qualities that textiles needed to have to be suitable for the stage. They had to be strong and durable but flexible enough so not to restrict movement. From the late '40s, I also became involved in making clothes for film and television, which again needed knowledge of different textiles and new techniques. In this new medium, we were learning all the time. It was important to know what lighting did to the colours and clothes and working this out was often a case of trial and error. I began to understand what was needed and learned to look at fabric differently. It wasn't long before my skills with textiles were noticed and I began to be asked to get more involved in its development, particularly in the world of industry.

For many years, I worked on a committee for the British Colour Council in the retail fashion service. These were interesting and absorbing days. The committee met in a charming house on Chandos Place, in the shadow of the BBC, and was chaired by Desmond Preston and later Cyril Kern. Information about colours used all over the world were collected and shown to the committee and it was our job to forecast the colour trends for the British fashion industry for the next two years. A look and a name had to be found for each chart before it was sent out to various trades. Many famous people worked on these committees. Several were permanent members and others were co-opted on a seasonal basis. Two of the most well known were the Daily Mail fashion writer, Iris Ashley, and the dress designer Charles Creed. Fashion advisers from many of the big stores, wholesale houses and international fashion magazines were also invited to give their expert opinions.

One frequent visitor to the colour studio was George Hopkinson. One day, George was discussing with Miss Battersby, the secretary and co-ordinator, the need to find new talent to lecture to the Bradford Textile Society and she suggested my name. George came to Lachasse to interview me and, from that moment, we became great friends and appreciated each other's capabilities. I spent most of my spare time over the next decade on visits to the North and Midlands, lecturing for various groups connected with the textile trade. These groups showed a great interest in the work I was doing to promote British design and the British fashion industry.

Princess Margaret took a great interest in the work of the Colour Council and served as Patron. From time to time, she paid us a visit to see how we were working. On one visit in 1967, the committee gathered in a room surrounded by colour charts and predictions with Her Royal Highness walking among us and asking questions. She took a keen interest in the charts, especially in the effect of lighting on the choices we were making. Later, we all had tea and she was able to talk to each member of the committee about his or her work in the fashion world. It was obvious that the Princess was keenly interested in the colours and textures of the moment and she always ask informed questions about our work. After many years, other organisations took up similar work and faced with rising costs it was decided to end the project, which had had a long and fruitful life.

I became involved in working for the Clothing Institute. We strived to keep the fashion trade informed of new colours, trends, innovations and of any problems facing the industry. I gave lectures at summer schools and at various events and, in

1965, I was made the Chairman of the design section, which had been formed to represent the interests of clothing designers. I became involved in all aspects of the Institute and all areas of textile. I even wrote book reviews for the Clothing Institute Journal. Some of the books I reviewed were based on the practical elements of fashion, some on the theory and some on the business side of the industry. Each one made me aware of the huge changes that were happening as a result of technology and the arrival of the computer. I came to realise that these were changes that could overnight affect thousands of textile workers.

The Clothing Institute organised many conventions and conferences throughout the '60s and I often took part and gave my predictions for the future of fashion. These events drew many great names from all branches of the fashion trade and beyond. In 1967, Teddy Tinling, once a famous tennis player, showed some of his original sportswear designs. Dr John Pomeroy, who was then working with Viyella International, Betty Williams of Berlei UK Ltd. and John Carr-Doughty also took part. Betty Williams was a great supporter of the conventions and we worked closely together for many years. We developed under-garments for evening gowns and tried to solve the never-ending problem of what to do with bra shoulder straps. The list of those who took part in the conventions is endless and includes such great names of fashion as Iris Ashley, then the fashion consultant to Peter Robinsons, Ailsa Garland, fashion co-ordinator for IPC Magazines, and Colin Woodhead, Group Merchandise and Fashion Co-ordinator for Austin Reed. The audience was made up of workers from every area of the trade who were seeking to gain knowledge from the professionals. These conventions, and the ideas and research that went into them, helped boost the industry in the '60s and '70s.

My work did not end there. In 1970, the post of Chief Examiner became vacant. Roy Godden, the Director of the Institute, asked me if I would take it up. This involved setting questions twice a year for examinations. These were sent in by other Institute members and it was my job to formulate the various design papers and make sure that they covered all areas of the fashion trade. The papers were then sent to the moderators and finally back to me before going to press. Then, when the examinations had been taken, the completed papers went to the other members for marking before being sent to me for the final assessment. It was a good deal of work and responsibility. I had to read every line carefully to make sure that the student had been given a fair assessment and either mark them up or down the scale. It was an arduous task and took around three weeks to complete before the final results could be sent to the governing body. In all, I had around 150 to 200 papers to mark twice a year. It was fascinating to see how the students from all over the English-speaking world answered the same questions. There was always huge variety in their replies.

Another job which fell to the Chairman of the Design section annually was to work with the committee of experts from all sections of the clothing trade and sift through nominations for the Fashion Writer of the Year, in both male and female categories. Many famous people in the industry won the awards, which were sponsored by the Singer Sewing Machine Company and ICI Fibres. It was often a difficult task but after hours of concentrated effort on all sides the annual winner slowly emerged. The presentations were made at places all over London. Sometimes they were held in the City, at the Merchant Taylors' Hall, at a hotel or in showrooms, like that of the International Wool Secretariat in Carlton Gardens or in the Lachasse showroom with a reception and a mini fashion show.

In September 1971, I was given the necessary approval by the Further and Higher Education Sub-Committee to become a governor of the Hammersmith College of Art and Building to represent the Clothing Institute. I enjoyed being a governor for several years and found it an interesting sideline to my own work. I was able to share the views of the commercial fashion world to those responsible for educating its future workers.

During my career, I saw many changes in the textile industry and was able to play a part fabric development. Whenever the fabric manufacturer Courtaulds produced a new fabric, they would commission Lachasse to make it up. We were asked to keep very careful notes and details of any problems we encountered during making the garment. It was a wonderful time as new lines and colours were flooding the market and we had to solve many new problems. Today, the modern woman takes easy care clothes for granted but I can remember when things weren't so easy. I recall when one of my clients asked Lachasse to make up a suit that she could put into a washing machine and the look of utter terror that spread through the showroom.

Through my own work as a designer and my responsibilities for helping predict and shape the future of fashion, I became fascinated by the demands on different textiles. I looked for inspiration everywhere and tried to acquire as much knowledge as possible, often from the most unlikely places. Through Norman Kent, one of my co-governors of the Hammersmith College of Art and Building, I was invited to visit the Wimpey Laboratories in Middlesex. It didn't at first appear to be a place connected with fashion design but there were some interesting challenges that work wear had to face.

I was met by Norman at the works gates and we began our tour. The very first thing that struck me was how very clean and tidy it all was. I had always imagined that when you worked in a foundry or on the shop floor there would be piles of rubbish, dirt and chaos everywhere. It was nothing like I had imagined. Here, the floors were swept almost as soon as the unwanted metal or rubber hit the ground. All the jigs and tools were in neat rows. There was activity everywhere. There were tyres that had been sent back from the Middle East to be retreaded and almost completely re-made. Mechanical shovels reached to the sky and wheels, which were designed for work in the desert, seemed to be as large as Piccadilly Circus.

Norman represented the Institute of Building and was proud of his work with the company and was keen to show me all the unusual sights of the laboratories. He took me to a row of experimental homes, which were used to try out all kinds of heating, including solar power. There was an artificial lagoon, where tidal waves were made in order to see the effect on harbour walls and beaches. I walked on bridges suspended over vast tanks, looked down on model docks that would have delighted any schoolboy, and was hurried out of the danger zone where the strength of an enormous steel girder was about to be put to the test. I saw a diver testing all kinds of materials in a tank and a library of sand, rocks and earth from every county of England. These were being tested so that the right foundations would be used in the making of roads and erection of buildings. I visited an outside greenhouse where tomato plants, cucumbers and marrows were flourishing, grown on chemicals alone.

I learned a great deal from this visit and began to understand the kind of clothing that was needed by men and women working in this kind of environment. I needed this information when I was asked by Dr Peter Ellis, who was organising a symposium on coated textiles at the University of Bradford in 1975, to design some garments and to talk about them at the event. It was held in conjunction with Storeys of Lancaster, who made four of my designs in their polyurethane-coated 'Maxella' fabric. I spoke about the design and the problems that had arisen in the construction of the garments. Then questions followed. At times, the chairman had his work cut out to keep order. Representatives from the fabric manufacturers were questioned about the durability of the garments and any practical problems they encountered. It was an exhausting but worthwhile session and gave me plenty to think about on my train journey home. I felt that we had all been able to learn from each other, in whatever field of the clothing industry we worked.

I was often invited to talk at Universities across the country on the subject of fashion and textiles. When Brian J Hill, who was working with the Lambeg Linen Research Association, became Senior Lecturer for Textiles and Chemistry at Ulster College, he suggested that I talk to his students. He was looking for someone who could give a lecture about the world of haute couture and what the fashion industry needed from those about to enter the industry. The knowledge and interest that these students showed overwhelmed me. The artistic taste that developed amid the troubles in Northern Ireland showed a longing to escape into a world of beauty and fantasy. I kept my connections to the college, and to Northern Irish design, and when a show was held at the Ulster offices of fabrics, I was delighted to show some of my designs alongside those of the Art and Design students. It was a small show aimed at the fashion trade at a time when unemployment was rising in Northern Ireland. It attracted great interest in the skills of the students, and in the industry in general, and we all hoped that this would lead to more long-term employment for people in the area.

My work did not go unnoticed and I was given many awards and commendations. In April 1972, I was awarded the Lemkin Medal by the Institute for my services to the Clothing Institute and this was presented to me at a ceremony held at the Cafe Royal, Regent Street.

Chapter Eighteen

America

In the late '60s, I was invited to a Christmas wedding in New York. It had always been my life-long ambition to go to America. I was of course thrilled by the invitation but the more I thought about it the more excuses I found for not going. I had recently bought a flat and had only just settled in. I was worried about leaving Lachasse and my teaching job for such a long trip. Going also meant that I would miss my family Christmas in Norfolk. I firmly decided against the trip.

My mother was staying with me that November, so I gave a dinner party in her honour. Over dinner, I mentioned the wedding invitation and explained all the reasons why I couldn't go. My mother realised at once that it was the chance of a lifetime and urged me to accept the invitation. An American friend at the dinner party, Sue John McLeod, was also in favour of me going. She was planning to travel to New York in December and was looking for a travelling companion. She offered to show me around New York and introduce me to her friends in exchange for us splitting all costs. The chance to follow my dream was too good to miss and so I accepted the invitation with only a few weeks to go. There were a million jobs to be carried out before leaving. There were Christmas cards that needed to be signed and envelopes addressed for my business and personal friends and packages that had to be posted. Somehow, I finished everything and was ready to go.

On 16th December, the day of my great adventure arrived. At the airport, I quickly realised one reason why Sue was so eager to have me as her travelling companion. When we checked in, my luggage was way under the permitted weight allowance while hers was very much above the limit. According to our agreement, I was obliged to pay half of her excess baggage costs. We were met at Kennedy Airport by a car and chauffeur and driven through New York and on to Newton, a town outside the city. The journey was idyllic and, as we drove, all the interesting buildings and sights were pointed out to me. It was a beautiful scene. Snow lightly dusted the fields and trees and everywhere looked ravishing in the winter sunlight.

We rested in Newton for six days and enjoyed the hospitality of our American hosts who lived in a charming farmhouse at the top of a hill, at the end of a road lined with maple trees. When they returned from business each afternoon, we were taken out to hotels and bars for drinks and meals. Slowly, the snow deepened and the roads became difficult to drive along. The radio gave a warning of a blizzard and Arctic conditions. Panic arose and we weren't sure we could make it back safely to New York. My travelling companion worked on the problem all day and at the last minute announced that she had found a car willing to pick us up and we left early the next day.

We certainly didn't let the weather spoil our great adventure and before long we were travelling again, this time from New York to New Jersey. Lachasse had a business arrangement with a firm called Spadea Syndicate Inc. in Milford, New Jersey. We sent sketches to them and they chose a selection for their pattern-making service. Many international dress houses did this and in return we were paid a small royalty. When Mr and Mrs Spadea found out that I was in America, they invited Sue and me to lunch at their country home. We hired a car and driver and after several hours we arrived at Milford but were unable to find the address we had been given. I went into the local drugstore and showed my rather grubby piece of paper with the address on it to the man behind the counter. He looked puzzled.

'Why,' he said, 'you are in the wrong state! You want Cottsville, Pennsylvania, and this is Cottsville, New Jersey!'

I returned to the car and explained our predicament, telephoned Jim Spadea at the mill, where the patterns were produced, explained what had happened and apologised. Guffaws of laughter came down the line.

'Don't worry. Just keep me posted on your progress and I will pass it on to Jean who will hold back the meal.'

We drove along the river towards the correct town and saw people of all ages skating and enjoying the winter weather. When we finally arrived at the mill we were given a hurried tour. Then, Jim climbed into his car and told our driver to follow him. In and out of the snow-covered woods and up and down the country roads we went until we came to a clearing where a substantial wooden house stood settled into the hillside. We parked the car and were taken across the road and up a winding snow-covered garden path to the house. We were greeted by the family and staff who had been expecting us since mid-day.

When we entered the dining room, my breath was taken away. It was beautiful. There were carpets, tapestries and furniture originally designed for European castles and housed in a setting that did them full justice. A log fire was blazing and an exquisite table was set for a Christmas luncheon. The meal was delicious and, once it was over and toasts were made, we moved to another drawing room where the hearth was ablaze with an even larger log fire. Coffee was served and the conversation flowed. Outside, the snow was worsening and we remembered that we had to be back in New Jersey that night. Telephone calls were made and we were assured that, once out of Milford, the roads to New Jersey were reasonable but that we should leave as soon as possible.

We made our slow winding journey back to New York, while reflecting on our trip so far. We watched the falling snow, while the lights of New York crept up on us. The journey into the city was like going to the North Pole, but slowly we winded our way through the streets and reached the Latin Quarter of West 75th Street. It was dark by the time we entered the apartment building and Sue and I were ushered into a lift with our luggage. We were staying with an artist friend who had agreed to share his studio flat. I remember this part of the trip as a wonderful experience but at the time it was pure hell. There was one bedroom, a large reception room and a studio with a small bed in one corner. I slept on this bed, while Sue slept on a large chaise longue in the reception room and our host slept in his own bedroom. There was a small kitchen and an even smaller bathroom. There was certainly none of the luxury which I had hoped to find in glamorous New York. We spent the next seven days there with our host eagerly showing me the sights of the Upper West Side, while Sue visited her friends on the Upper East Side.

One luxuriously lazy afternoon, I was taken by one of my hostesses to a grand hotel where we drank tea and listened to the orchestra. We decided to have a cocktail before we faced the snow storm outside. My hostess ordered bourbon and I ordered a pink gin, a drink I discovered when I was a student at Chelsea. The waiter dashed backwards and forwards and we waited patiently. I tried several times to catch his eye without success. When I finally did get his attention, he muttered something about not having any pink gin in stock. I asked instead for gin, angostura bitters and a jug of water, which he quickly fetched. When they arrived, I started to fill my glass with these ingredients and announced to the confused waiter that this was a pink gin. Could it be that he had never heard about Noel Coward, pink gin or the '30s?

The week leading up to the wedding day was filled with endless parties, dances and family get-togethers. It seemed to me that the whole of New York was in some way engaged in a great celebration. At one of the many parties, I met the announcer Harry Fleetwood who, in 1969, became the raconteur and host of 'Music Through the Night' on WNCN-FM, New York's finest classical station. From the start, Harry and I got along well and he would tease me endlessly whenever we met. When I returned to London, I met him at a dinner party where I was talking to the other guests about my visit to New York. I mentioned that a friend of mine lived in a rather grotty area of New York and had thrown me a supper party when I was there.

Slowly, Harry smiled and in his quiet, dry way said, 'But, Peter, that is where I live and it was I who gave you that party!'

For once, I was the silent one.

On Christmas Eve, I went to a service in St Bartholomew's Cathedral. It was a moving experience of dignity in a fast-moving city of commerce. On Christmas Day, I joined Mrs Edna Rothschild and her family for present giving and a luncheon back on the Upper East Side. Then, it was back to the studio flat for a quick rest and to change my clothes before going back to the Upper East Side, where I joined the Hulton family, who had become great friends of mine when they lived in London. We celebrated Christmas and ate roast beef and Yorkshire pudding before, exhausted and overfed, I went to bed.

The wedding took place at the Unitarian Church of All Souls on Sunday 28th December. It was unforgettable. The church looked magnificent as we entered it from the ice cold winter's day. We left the snow behind to find the church decorated with hundreds of spring flowers, which had been flown in. The reception at the Hotel Pierre was like a fairy tale. The scene was pure splendour and we danced until dawn, when the bride and groom left for their honeymoon.

On New Year's Eve, I went to the Mark Hellinger Theatre to see Katherine Hepburn play Coco Chanel. I had been eager to attend the theatre in New York and this show didn't disappoint. I was interested to learn that the sets and costumes were designed by Cecil Beaton, who at one stage of his career had commissioned costumes from Lachasse for productions on the London stage. We drank the New Year in at the Waldorf Astoria and then, with the two children of Fritz Peters, the author of 'Finisterre', we watched the firework display amid the snow in Central Park.

It was soon time for Sue to leave New York and join her family in Texas and for me to fend for myself. As soon as Sue was in the taxi heading for the airport, I started to telephone my many friends in the city. I had thought that New York had turned itself inside out before the wedding but it was nothing compared what happened now that I was alone.

I was given a luncheon in my honour by Barbara Slipha at Orsini's, the Italian restaurant. This event led to many more invitations. One guest was the editor of Harper's Bazaar and gave me a personally guided tour of the Harper's Bazaar building and offices. Elliseva Sayers, a publicity agent in New York with excellent contacts had many invitations to keep me entertained. To start with, she arranged an invitation to a party given by Gloria Vanderbilt and her husband at their charming Manhattan town house. I still have a clear picture of Gloria standing in a black and white evening gown with her husband alongside wearing a patchwork waistcoat. The house was opened for all guests in order to launch her patchwork project, which was in evidence all around us. We were given a tour of the house and then shown into the dining room for a buffet supper. It was more like a Roman banquet than any buffet I had seen before. I still have a walnut the size of a tangerine, which she gave me from the centrepiece on the table when I left. It was a happy evening spent beside the large decorated Christmas tree while watching the snow falling outside.

Elliseva was organising a fashion show at the Jade Room of the Waldorf Astoria, to which I was invited. She introduced me to a great many people in the New York fashion world, including the Portuguese designer, Maria Theresa. I was curious to see how different a New York fashion show was from one in London. I was astonished when I went back stage to witness the final preparations to find a lack of organisation compared to the shows I had become used to in London. The elegant international mannequins were hunting for matching shoes in a large cardboard box. It was quite unlike the neat rows of shoes that we laid out before the start of our London shows. Despite this, it was a glossy affair and I wished that I could have booked many of the mannequins to work for the next collection at Lachasse.

During my trip, I did all the things that visitors do in New York. I viewed the Hudson River from the top of the Empire State Building. I went to the Frick art collection and spent hours gazing at its treasures. Unlike most other tourists, I also spent a long time watching the various salesgirls in Bergdorf Goodman. I noted their selling techniques and studied the clothes on sale. I became enchanted by the huge New York department stores. Whenever I arranged a rendezvous for lunch or cocktails, I would insist on meeting inside the main doors at Tiffany & Co.

All too soon, after all the excitement, the parties and the kindness of New York, it was time to leave. As I boarded the plane for London, I vowed to return just as soon as I could. I was lucky enough to do so several more times during my career. In 1972, I had the unusual honour of having an American road named after me by a friend who was financing part of a building project. Peter Lewis Crown Street is on an estate in the Pocono Mountains in Monroe County, Pennsylvania. Crossing Peter Lewis Crown Street is Pont Street, which my friend told me was to remind him of his many visits to my home on Pont Street, London.

Chapter Nineteen

The TT Rider

On my fiftieth birthday, I decided to break a childhood promise and buy myself a motorcycle. All my life I had longed for one but, as I already had a weak back, I was told that I could never ride a motorcycle. I made a solemn promise that I would not buy one but now I realised that it had always been one of my unfulfilled ambitions.

My brother had motorcycles when I was growing up and it was with great envy that I would watch him ride around Hunstanton and dash off to see friends in Surrey. In the mid '60s, I often visited friends who lived in Port Erin on the Isle of Man. The husband was a flag marshal in the TT races and on one occasion I went to stay during race week and joined a party of young men about my age. Our hostess had packed a hamper full of goodies for us all and we were taken to the starting enclosure. It was the greatest fun. We met all the motorcycle stars, including Mike Halewood and the young Agostini. I envied them as they dashed here and there. When I got back to the mainland, I became quite a regular fan at the Crystal Palace race track until it was closed and turned into a sports stadium.

In March each year, an accountant came to Lachasse and worked on the books and figures for the previous twelve months. For several years, one young accountant always arrived on his motorcycle and parked it in the little courtyard outside. One day, the longing to ride it overcame me and I begged him to take me for a spin. We met in a mews nearby, so that staff and clients could not see me if I fell off. I borrowed a crash helmet and jacket and off we set, to my horror, towards Park Lane and the heavy traffic. We sped through the park, weaving in and out of the traffic, towards Marble Arch and then round and back down Park Lane. I was thrilled and afterwards could think of nothing else but owning a bike of my own. I consulted many people, listened to their advice and eventually, on April 18th 1980, I awoke and decided that that was the day. I had lived fifty glorious years now I was going to live dangerously.

Cheque book in hand, I headed towards Kensington High Street and my dream bike. I knew exactly the bike I wanted and expected to take it out of the shop and ride it straight home. I soon found that I had to wait several weeks before all the necessary papers were completed and returned and insurance arranged. I had never had anything mechanical in my life, apart from my wrist watch, so needed some help. When the bike was ready, I asked the trade van from Lachasse to collect the bike and bring it to Farm Street. The young accountant had promised to give me lessons and so on the next Saturday I was up bright and early and off to meet him at Lachasse.

My teacher was late and so, to pass the time, I read the instructions in the manual, which I had brought years ago when staying on the Isle of Man. It all seemed so simple that I rashly mounted the bike. In a flash, it flew out around the courtyard, narrowly missing the large garage doors, and into the little street. Somehow, I managed to stop it and fell off in the process. A passerby rushed up to see if I was injured. I got up, more surprised than anything else. I wheeled the bike slowly back to Lachasse, having learned my lesson, and waited patiently for my teacher.

For several weeks, the accountant would come to Farm Street at weekends and patiently show me what to do and explain where I was going wrong. Eventually, it was time for me to leave Berkeley Square and venture into the traffic by myself. So the next Saturday, I went into the Mall only to be faced with the mounted cavalry going to the Changing of the Guard. I held on, tried to remember all I had been taught, and somehow passed them by safely.

Later, I joined a club for more lessons. We met each Saturday for a lecture and then were taken into the heavy traffic on the nearby roads. On one Saturday, the teacher took us out in the most terrible thunderstorm to teach us how to control our machines in bad conditions. We reached a roundabout when his bike, being very powerful, shot off and disappeared. I saw two large articulated lorries entering the roundabout, so gave way. When it was clear for me to enter, there was no sign of our teacher so I went in the direction I thought he had taken. On and on I went, with the twenty other learners following behind me and suddenly the instructor came flying up to me, scarlet in the face. We were all led quietly back to the school.

On another occasion, we had a lesson on balance in a playground. Cones were placed in rows and one by one we had to ride in and out, round and round, until I could see nothing but fluorescent cones coming towards me. It was at this lesson that I made up my mind that this kind of training was not for me. Instead of riding around in the playground, doing what we were told, we should have been taught to be patient, wait our turn and not cut in and out of the traffic. At some of the classes we were taught how to maintain our machines. We were supposed to take our motorcycle apart but the daunting prospect of finding the original homes for all those nuts and bolts convinced me to leave that kind of thing to the professionals.

I enjoyed riding my motorcycle for a number of years and it was the perfect way to relax after a busy week at Lachasse. Whenever I needed a breath of Norfolk air I dashed off, regardless of the weather conditions. I realised that to ride a motorbike well, I needed some of the same qualities for my career in fashion – a terrific capacity for hard work, boundless energy and determination. I never did ride my bike in the TT races, but at least I did achieve one of my life's great ambitions and gained tremendous satisfaction and happiness.

Chapter Twenty

The Future of Fashion

I am continually asked by people to try and predict the future of fashion but, like everything else in this uncertain world, it is always changing. During my long career in fashion, I have seen great diversity. New designers are born, new fabrics are developed and fashions come and go. Since the end of the Second World War and the start of my career, life has certainly changed. Labour has become expensive, birth rates have risen and leisure time has expanded.

All these have forced the public to demand different styles and types of clothing from previous generations. As travel by car has increased, the need for a topcoat has greatly diminished. Heavy garments are no longer necessary indoors because of central heating. Sadly, the occasions for elegant dressing are becoming fewer and clothing has become more casual. For instant amusement, we need only switch on the television and so people often relax on the sofa wearing casual clothes rather than dressing up to go to the theatre, cinema or other entertainment outside the home. The popularity for eating ready-prepared food means that we have less need to dress up and dine out so often.

These changes have not only affected the type of clothes people wear but also the fabric from which they are made. With the development of new synthetic fibres and chemical dyes, fabrics and colours have lost the subtleties of bygone ages. They are now bold and sometimes crude, quite unlike the delicate beauty of traditional textiles. With the increase in international travel, it has become necessary for clothing to weigh less and take up less space and so lightweight synthetic materials have become popular. New types of clothing have been developed for new purposes, particularly in the world of sport. The need for less restrictive and specialist garments for leisure pursuits has given fashion a new market.

The fashion industry has changed enormously since I began my career. The influence of catwalk models has meant that many people use the fashion industry to advertise themselves in the hope of winning lucrative contracts from companies, selling anything from cosmetics and jewellery to cars. Advertising and branding now play a huge part in the industry and everyone is trying to sell something and it is no longer just about the clothes.

The way people value clothes has also changed. I feel that most of the young people of today, who claim that they want to express their individuality, are all unkempt, untidy and messy. They refuse to set any kind of standard but still expect all the privileges previously connected to social behaviour or dress. Many have great sympathy with the underprivileged of other countries and to show this they seem to adopt their way of dressing, while quite forgetting that originally many styles of clothing were born out of necessity due to climate and culture. The great urge to level all humans to one standard, regardless of need or lifestyle, has become popular. Women seem to no longer wish to look outstanding, as they once did, but instead they buy clothes to blend into the background. There is now instant fashion, which is led from the streets and no longer from stage and film stars. People are now more independent and self assured and, as a result, the high standards of fashion are slipping.

The art and skill needed to create couture clothes is dying out due to modern technology and the desperate desire for speed. People now only seem interested in wearing clothing covered with logos to display their wealth, whereas in the past designing, cutting and skilful handling of material was much more important. Modern machinery and technology have replaced the love and devotion that used to go into each garment as speed and profit have taken over. People no longer give the time to fittings and can't wait for their clothes to be specially made and instead want them instantly.

I have given the future direction of fashion a great deal of thought and have arrived at several possibilities. I am sure that fashion will change and adapt just as it has always done to fit new environments and the needs of society. Perhaps lifestyle, through necessity, will force changes in fashion and climate change will alter the way we look at clothing. In the future, perhaps as the temperature rises due to climate change, people will start to wear body paint as a form of fashion. Temperature, war, the lack of supplies could be the greatest influential factor. Social changes and the ups and downs of employment could bring a revolution in the garment industry. There are so many possible scenarios that could change fashion forever.

This is a challenging time for students entering the fashion market. I fear that many young people today are only interested in designing clothes for their own age group. They forget that there is a large, and wealthy, market of people who have top jobs and need clothes that flatter and give them confidence. The couture end of fashion will give these newcomers an interesting life and a chance to meet some fascinating people. They can make a good living while being less exposed to mass commercialism than in mainstream fashion. They will certainly not become wealthy, as many seem to hope, and it will be hard work. Not everyone will reach the top of the trade and not all are suited. For those who fall by the wayside, it will be for the best. All the experiences they gain will lead to another career in one of the many areas of the fashion industry, which at the outset they might not have envisaged.

I have spent my whole life working in fashion and it has been both extremely hard work and immensely fulfilling. Once, I was asked what I did to relax after my work and replied truthfully that I never relaxed. Once in this trade, you live clothes. To be successful in fashion, you must give it your all. Luckily, I always knew what I wanted from my life and set out to obtain it by gradual means. I worked long, tiring hours and often held several jobs simultaneously. For me, life has been happy, sometimes sad and worrying, but always a fascinating journey. At the very least, I know that I have tried and succeeded in doing what I was born to do. It is now time for me to step back and watch with interest everything that happens next in the fashion world.